It's a Wired World

It's a Wired World
The New Networked Economy

Anne C. Leer

SCANDINAVIAN UNIVERSITY PRESS
Oslo – Stockholm – Copenhagen – Oxford – Boston

Scandinavian University Press (Universitetsforlaget AS)
P.O. Box 2959 Tøyen, N-0608 Oslo, Norway
Fax +47 22 57 53 53
URL: http:/www.scup.no

Stockholm office
SCUP, Scandinavian University Press
P.O. Box 3255, S-103 65 Stockholm, Sweden

Copenhagen office
Scandinavian University Press AS
P.O. Box 54, DK-1002 København K, Denmark

Oxford office
Scandinavian University Press UK
60 St. Aldates, Oxford OX1 1ST, England

Boston office
Scandinavian University Press North America
875 Massachusetts Ave., Ste. 84, Cambridge MA 02139, USA
Fax +1 617 354 6875

© Scandinavian University Press (Universitetsforlaget AS), Oslo 1996
and ECSC – EEC – EAEC, Brussels-Luxembourg, 1996

ISBN 82-00-42310-7

This book has been published in collaboration with the European Commission,
Directorate General XIII, Telecommunications, Information Market and
Exploitation of Research, with particular support from the Information
Engineering Sector. However, the responsibility for the content remains with the
author and the European Commission is not accountable for any statements or
information given.

All rights reserved. No part of this publication may be reproduced, stored in a
retrieval system, or transmitted, in any form or by any means, electronic,
mechanical, photocopying, recording, or otherwise, without the prior
permission of Scandinavian University Press. Enquiries should be sent to the
Rights Department, Scandinavian University Press, Oslo, at the address above.

Design: Astrid Elisabeth Jørgensen
Cover illustration: © NPS/nonstøck/Theo Barten
Illustrations: David Keeping
Typeset in 11.5 on 13 point Photina by
Heien Fotosats A.s, Norway
Printed on 90 gms Partner Offset ∞ by SRT A.s, Norway

"We are all great abbreviators. None of us has the wit to know the whole truth, the time to tell it if we believed we did, or an audience so gullible as to accept it."
Aldous Huxley, *Brave New World*, 1932

Contents

Foreword by Dr Martin Bangemann, European Commission   1
Hello there, Reader, ... 3
Acknowledgements 5

Introduction 7

1 CONTEXT 11
    The shrinking planet 11
       The development of media and communication
       technologies 12
       Innovation and the rate of change 17
       Towards the Knowledge Age 19
    The rise of the global information infrastructure (GII) ... 22
       The US information superhighway: the US NII
       Agenda for Action and GII Agenda for Co-operation .. 23
       The European approach 26
       Initiatives in Asia 28
       The developing world 30
    Visions of the global information society 31
       Emerging global systems 35

2 THE BUSINESSS CHALLENGE 42
    Hype versus reality 42
    The search for a market 46
       The problem of sizing the market 48

The Content Race	54
The meaning of convergence	57
The Strategic Alliance Syndrome	59
The new evolving market structure	60
Redefining the market	62
Challenges and strategic responses of key players	64
The public sector	64
The private sector	69
The changing world of advertising	69
The changing world of publishing	73
Understanding process and managing bits	80
Changing business models	85

3 CONTENT MANAGEMENT AND INTELLECTUAL PROPERTY RIGHTS ... 89

Trading information and media as digital bits	89
The trouble with information assets	90
The intellectual property system	92
Copyright: the critical trading mechanism of the global information market	94
The origin of copyright	97
Copyright in the international environment	99
The Berne Convention	100
The Universal Copyright Convention	100
Legislation in the mould	103
Copyright as a trade mechanism	104
Copyright as an object of trade	105
The current system of copyright administration and clearance	106
The Anglo-American model of reproduction rights organisation	107
The German-Spanish model	108
The Dutch model	108
The Nordic model	108

The role of collecting societies in an electronic
environment 109

4 ELECTRONIC COMMERCE AND INFORMATION TRANSACTIONS 111
What makes the market work 111
Information transactions defined 112
The security challenge 114
    Cryptography and the use of encryption technology .. 115
    Emerging standards for encrypting information 116
    Information encoding and identifiers 119
Transactional systems for network commerce 121
    Existing and emerging transactional mechanisms and models: subscription and licensing, credit and debit cards, smart cards, third-party clearing and brokering, electronic cash, electronic cheques 122
    Electronic Data Interchange (EDI) 132

5 THE WAY FORWARD 134
Summary of critical issues 134
    Digital information transactious 134
    Changing markets and new business models 135
    Information identification and the protection of IPRs 136
    Copyright protection and rights clearance 136
    Security versus privacy 137
    The legal and regulatory jungle 138
    Global information society versus information city states 139
Conditions for market efficiency, and potential risks 140
    Less choice 141
    Back to proprietary systems 141
    Deregulation leading to monopolistic competition 141
    Lack of security 142
    Infringement of privacy and consumer rights 142

Loss of right to information access and universal
service 142
Barriers to overcome 143
Projections of future developments 145
The individual citizen and the wired wrorld 146

Appendices 149
1 Chapter 1 of the Bangemann Report, *Europe and the
   Global Information Society: Recommendations to the
   European Council*, 26 May 1994 149
2 Speech of US Vice President Al Gore at the
   International Telecommunications Union's first
   World Telecommunication Development
   Conference, Buenos Aires, March 1994 161
3 List of documents on the information society and
   infrastructure released by national governments,
   the European Commission and G7 countries 174
Notes 177
Select bibliography 181
Glossary 183

Foreword

The technical revolution of the 21st century caused by new electronic and digital technology has substantial impacts on our economy as well as on our society. Industry is facing challenges in finding new markets, new business strategies, new ways of organising labour or new forms of international co-operation.

The impacts of this technical development on our social and our private lives are of equal importance. The population will have a wider range of possibilities for communication and interchange of information and data. However, people must be prepared for the use and application of the information technology: Education, training, "life-long learning" will become vital, particularly with regards to the labour market.

There is no doubt that new qualified jobs will be created in the information society. To exploit this opportunity and to ensure the appropriate education and training of people, political, economic and social priority should be given to these issues.

The global flow and interchange of information and data requires data protection, protection of property rights and protection of the private sphere: A legal framework is of substantial importance to stimulate private investment and to provide incentives to market development. It is also important to instil user confidence in the new technology.

It is the politician's role to define a legal basis for the information society. Within the European Union we have already made important steps in that direction. The task of the entrepreneurs is to make the wired world a reality, thus finding new markets, new applications and areas for new job creation.

We are unable to project the "new face" of the wired world because of the complexity of the challenges we are facing. Therefore it is of vital importance to discuss the new subjects, to interchange both ideas and experience. This book will offer facts, ideas and stimulation because it presents a wide range of important themes, and as such is a contribution to the global debate about the information society.

Dr Martin Bangemann,
Commissioner of the European Commission
9 September 1996
Brussels

Hello there, Reader,

I'm Anne the Author and if this book had been published online, we could have continued this conversation. You could have said something like "pleased to meet you" and I could have asked you why you bought my book and, later, asked you if you had actually read it and if you liked it. You would have been able to ask me questions and correct me if you thought I got it all wrong. You could have e-mailed me instant feedback such as "I think your book stinks!" or, preferably, something more like "I loved your book from beginning to end!"

In spite of its subject-matter, this book will reach you in a form to be read in linear mode and I shall have to cope without your wholesome feedback. It seems that you and I still have some time to wait before we can meet online and indulge in real-time communication as author and reader.

Although I find it exciting that one day you and I will be able to meet and exchange our digital bits via electronic means, I must confess I do not understand how we are supposed to cope with the promised interactive capability of future applications. I don't know about you, but for me finding the time could prove to be difficult. I have great difficulty today, even before all this interactive technology descends upon us, in finding enough time to communicate with all the people I want to communicate with.

I also suffer from that modern executive disease "chronic information guilt" caused by never having enough time to update myself and read all those useful documents that have been prepared and sorted for me. It really makes me wonder how on earth we will find the time in the future to use all that knowledge at our fingertips, the myriad of communication tools and interactive applications that are currently being developed. If you have the answer to that after reading this book I would love to hear from you!

I suspect that in future, the challenge of competition will be not so much about different technologies and applications, but about people's time, their need for functionality and their desire for convenience.

In the meantime, I hope you enjoy the book and find it of some practical use in whatever domain you happen to be. And if you really want to talk to me, I would be happy to receive your email – you can find me at the following address: leera@oup.co.uk.

Acknowledgements

Books are never created by the author alone – and this book is certainly no exception. Many people past and present have influenced and shaped this work – it would be a very long list if they were all to be acknowledged by name. So, I shall refrain from doing so and restrict the list to those who played a major role in making it possible for me to write this book.

This book would not have been written had it not been for the positive encouragement of Bernard Smith at the European Commission in Luxembourg, the support of Dr Richard B. Scott and the patience of my colleagues at Oxford University Press, whose support and professional insights I greatly appreciate.

I would also like to extend my gratitude to my editor Bjørn Gunnar Saltnes for his enthusiasm and for knowing what to say at those critical junctures. To my dear friend Michelle Leer I give a big non-virtual hug for just being there when needed – thanks for your solid support. To Anni and Michael Delahaye, thank you providing the perfect setting for writing this book at your medieval retreat in the South of France. I felt honoured to be the first ever Internet connection in that ancient village. It was fantastic sitting on the terrace of the old château, overlooking the green valley, with my digital mobile phone downloading files from the US Library of Congress in America and transmitting new chapters back to England. Being connected to the wired world suddenly became useful and exciting. But somehow I hope that your village will never change and that digitised souls like me will still have somewhere to go in the future where we can be put back together again . . .

To all of you who have given me input and inspirations along the way: Thanks!

Introduction

Pick up virtually any magazine or newspaper these days and you will be told, by advertising or editorial, that the electronic future is here. This is a future in which the world will run on digital communications networks, fibre optic cables and satellites, in which your home will become an 'interactive information/entertainment centre', your office a filling station on the 'electronic highway' – and everything from your bank to your backache will be processed through a computer.[1]

These words were written back in 1983, but in fact this statement rings just as true today. Evidently, delivering the promises of the much-heralded Information Society takes a long time. Rome wasn't built in a day; contrary to popular opinion, learning how to utilise progress takes time.

The cheerleaders and promoters of the wired world have called for our immediate response to the information revolution for well over three decades now. If it is a revolution, it must be the longest-running one in history.

Perhaps the sense of urgency is misguided. Don't get me wrong, by now nobody should dispute the essential importance of taking part in the development of the global information society. Our nations' competitiveness depends on our involvement. But, many organisations are rushing into action for the wrong reasons and without clear objectives, driven by a sense of panic and fear of being left behind. It may be good to get on to the learning curve earlier rather than later, but it can also prove to be very expensive: "Experience is a good teacher, but she sends in terrific bills."[2]

Managers often feel pressured to be seen to be doing something in the electronic domain and consequently allow their organisations to dip a toe into experimental waters. Active research, experimentation and pilot projects are essential activities for any organisation that wants to be competitive in a changing market. However, more often, the toe-dipping is something managers do rather reluctantly with no real enthusiasm for what is new, and without any long-term commitment to research and development. Toe-dipping in a few digital waters can be a welcome escape strategy, designed to make management and shareholders alike feel comfortable, rather than entrepreneurial. It can lull managers into an operational sleep mode where they believe they can carry on more or less as before and where no one will force them to face up to any major decisions about digital opportunities.

Experimentation that does not have full management backing and funding often fails, so providing examples of "lots of expenditure for nothing", quoted whenever research and development are on the agenda.

The need to get properly involved is urgent for those who want to be competitive or who want to be in the driving seat when they take part. Organisations and individuals who haven't already done so should really go for a deep dive into those digital waters and submerge themselves in all the new opportunities flooding our way. But a word of warning: don't go diving before you know how to swim and don't set sail before you know how to navigate. Read this book first. And maybe a few others too, as this one can only offer you a very small part of a big story.

The real urgency is that we need to invest resources in the understanding of change and to develop strategies designed to take advantage of these changes. Haste, combined with short-term vision and fragmented thinking, is a widespread contemporary disease – Hastomania fragmentalis. We need to focus more clearly on what exactly it is we want to achieve, rather than allow technological events and shifting market pressures dictate our direction. Throwing huge sums of money at anything with the words "digital" or "information technology" on it, will save neither the world nor corporate profits.

Buying a multimedia PC in order to improve your child's education will not guarantee educational success or turn your child into a high achiever. Owning a piece of technology does not deliver instant results. Technology is at best merely a mean to an end, not the end itself. Technology delivers tools designed with a particular purpose in mind. But the purpose is defined by human intelligence and ambition, not technology. Technology itself is dead. It only comes alive through human intervention. The interesting challenge is the application and extension of all the various tools technology is providing us with.

To reap the benefits of technology we need to know what we want to achieve, understand the applications of various technologies, find the appropriate tools and learn to master them.

Results will depend upon how the technology is being used, the content and support available and who the individual user is. The individual user's skills and capacity for interaction with available content and tools are critical factors for success. The most significant dependent variables on the chart of success are not of a technological, but a human nature. Whether your child will benefit from using a multimedia PC will depend much more on the quality of the learning environment and on the content, rather than the technology and mechanics, of operation.

Similarly, providing all your employees with Internet connections will not guarantee the company a secure future or deliver any instant results beyond a significantly larger telephone bill. Investing in a GSM mobile telephone may make you more available and give you that ego-boosting feeling of being very well connected. But it will not make you instantly more productive. Even the cutting edge of digital telecommunications will not change your ability to generate economic value. Only you can do that.

However, enough of technological scepticism. It is happening: the "electronic future" is here, at least in terms of technical achievements. Information technology has invaded our environment and its influence will continue to spread, probably without us even noticing. It is a matter of fact that digital communication networks will cover the globe before long and bring significant changes to most aspects of society.

Those of us who have been around long enough, or have bothered to look into its history, will know that the concept of the Information Society is not a new one. Wise political leaders, philosophers and writers of the past have seen the importance of intellectual creations and information as fundamental to the acquisition of power, to economic growth and to social benefits.

In all parts of our society, people are talking of transformation and the need to master the process of change. But there seems to be much confusion as to exactly what the scope and value of these changes are and what the implications are beyond the short term. Furthermore, the rate of change is typically exaggerated, as the quotation at the start of this Introduction clearly demonstrates. It doesn't take the artist long to buy the paint, but it takes considerable knowledge, talent and a very long time to master the art.

So, how far have we come, what impact have digital technologies had on our society, and how much really has changed? Chapter 1 recapitulates a little history, establish what the status of the Information Society is today and what are the key issues on the current agenda. The overview this provides will be a useful backdrop for the chapters that follow.

Chapter 1
Context

The shrinking planet

The impact of advances in information technology, communications and media can be summed up in one sentence. Quite literally, the world has shrunk. A manufacturing company based in Wales can finance its operations in the United States, run production in remote parts of China, assemble in Denmark and ship from Germany, and vice versa. The country of origin has become the world of origin.

The application of communication networks and digital technologies has changed the constraints of time and space, shifted geographical and industrial borders, and reduced the importance of physical location. Time, location and national jurisdictions still matter, and will continue to do so. They will not be eradicated by the digital network revolution, as some digital believers suggest. What is happening is change, not disappearance.

Computer technology is all around and has transformed our lives – the way we do business, conduct scientific research, provide education, practise medicine, create art, how we run the country, preserve our history, travel from one place to another, function at home, how we communicate with one another, and so on. Business correspondence that used to take days to deliver is now instantly communicated via fax or email. Newsworthy events from around the world are transmitted live into our homes as and when they happen. Scientists publish and discuss their research in global networks. Children do their homework on personal computers using Internet. Doctors supervise operations remotely through telemedicine networks without having to be physically present in the theatre. People can stay in touch and access global networks from anywhere in the world using digital mobile phones. Supermarkets operating across national borders accumulate detailed records of individual customers' shopping patterns – who buys what, when, and where.

All these new ways of living our lives and conducting business have come about as a result of technological invention. But the wired world of today is a very young child of human history. By recent estimates, our planet is over 4,000 million years old and the first human beings walked the Earth approximately 300,000 years ago.[3] Yet, most technology has been invented and evolved over the past five hundred years of human history and computer technology in particular only over the past hundred years or so. However, it does not follow from this that people were not creative, or did not value information and knowledge, before the advent of new technology.

The development of media and communication technologies

In technical terms, the history of electronic media and communication technology started with the inventions of the printing press and the telegraph. The telegraph was patented in 1837, in England by the physicist Sir Charles Wheatstone and in the United States by the inventor Samuel F.B. Morse, who had both discovered the communication capabilities of electricity.[4] The first telegraph line in the United States was commissioned by Congress by giving Morse $30,000 to set up a line between Washington DC and Baltimore. His first successful demonstration was sending the message: "What hath God wrought!" on 24 May 1844. That was some four hundred years after Gutenberg printed the first publication in 1442 on his new printing press and subsequently established "mass printing" as a market reality.

The inventions of the printing press and telegraph have nothing in common in terms of technology. However, they are strongly connected in that each provided a cornerstone for the later development of electronic media and communication technology. Together, these two separate events were to lay down the foundations for three major media industries: print publishing, telephony and broadcasting. These technologies evolved as separate disciplines for over two centuries before converging towards the end of the 1970s into a multidisciplinary process.

Today print is under challenge as the dominant media for distributing information. Communication technology has developed from the telegraph to the radio, telephone, photography, film and television. And most significant of all has been the arrival of the computer and digital technologies, bringing fundamental changes across the media and communication industries.

The last decade has seen several technical breakthroughs that are causing an upheaval in the media and communication industries:

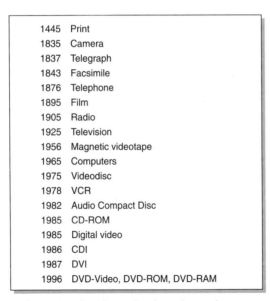

1445	Print
1835	Camera
1837	Telegraph
1843	Facsimile
1876	Telephone
1895	Film
1905	Radio
1925	Television
1956	Magnetic videotape
1965	Computers
1975	Videodisc
1978	VCR
1982	Audio Compact Disc
1985	CD-ROM
1985	Digital video
1986	CDI
1987	DVI
1996	DVD-Video, DVD-ROM, DVD-RAM

Figure 1   Development of media technology: key milestones
© A. Leer/Scandinavian University Press, 1996

in particular, advances in semiconductor, video, cable and satellite technology, such as digital video, fibre optics, broadband transmission, ASDL, ATMs, high-speed cables, modems, and a range of satellite equipment. The way in which today we produce and distribute media content would have seemed like science fiction to someone living only ten years ago.

Although the different media has developed in separate traditions, they have from the very start been very strongly influenced by each other. As Marshall McLuhan put it, "The content of any new medium is an older medium."[5] The first print publishers were influenced by pre-print media – professional communicators such as the storyteller, the messenger, the preacher, the teacher, the entertainer. These ancient forms are now coming back in the shape of intelligent agents and other mediating characters in multimedia publishing.

The printing press is significant for an appreciation of how the media have evolved as an industry. The printing press permitted the development of mass-print publishing, which constituted the first major change of medium of communication into a complex business operation. Print publishing, in particular newspaper publishing, had a substantial influence on television. But although the influence is still there, it has diminished over the years as television has developed into a major media industry in its own right. For the past decade or two, it has been more popular to study the impact of television upon newspapers than vice versa.

Today print is still the most widespread, established and distributed medium. The professionals of the printing press developed a tradition that provided the frame of reference for broadcasters when they arrived on the scene half a century later.

The first radio broadcasters copied the recipes of the newspaper format: a blend of news, reports and commentaries, sports and entertainment. In fact entertainment was the chosen market application for the first radio broadcast and first television broadcast. And entertainment has continued to be the most important application for broadcasting – an exception being during the

Second World War, when radio was used by the German Nazis to control and direct the nation and by the British and their allies to inform and provide moral support to their people.

In the course of the evolution of the media industry, every time a new medium was invented, it was first rejected, and seen as a threat to the existing media. People thought the telephone was a stupid idea and were not impressed when, in March 1876, Alexander Graham Bell reported the world's first successful telephone call: "Mr Watson, come here, I want you." Who would use such a silly contraption?

The British film-maker Sir David Puttnam reminds us that "It took the movie business twenty years to develop into anything approaching a serious medium in its own right. For those first two decades it was busily dismissed as much ado about nothing, a gimmick, even just a new source of depravity – just as some of the more inflated claims about the current communications revolution are dismissed today."

Even when writing was first introduced in Egypt during the 4th century BC, it was rejected. The story goes that one day King Thamus of Egypt had a visit from Theuth, who presented him with the invention of writing, saying, "Here is an accomplishment, my lord the King, that will improve both the wisdom and the memory of the Egyptians."

But King Thamus replied, "Theuth, my paragon of inventors, the discoverer of an art is not the best judge of the good or harm which will accrue to those who practise it. So it is in this; you, who are the father of writing, have out of fondness for your offspring, attributed to it quite the opposite of its real function. Those who acquire it will cease to exercise their memory and become forgetful; they will rely on writing to bring things to their remembrance by external signs instead of their own internal resources. What you have discovered is a receipt for recollection, not for memory. And as for wisdom, your pupils will have the reputation for it without the reality: they will receive a quantity of information without proper instruction, and in consequence be thought very knowledgeable when they are for the most part ignorant. And because they are filled with the conceit of wisdom instead of real wisdom they will be a burden to society"[6]

King Thamus was right; but he was also terribly wrong. Technology is a two-edged sword. In our day, Neil Postman, a frequent commentator on the state of our information society, is warning us about the "one-eyed prophets who see only what new technologies can do and are incapable of imagining what they will undo. ...It is a mistake to suppose that any technological innovation has a one-sided effect. Every technology is both a burden and a blessing; not either-or, but this-and-that."[7]

Those who thought television would be the end of the cinema, and that computers would kill the book, have been proven wrong. And when Nicholas Negroponte predicts the end of the peer-reviewed scientific journal in printed form, because the online electronic journal will replace it, he sounds like yet another one-eyed prophet.[8]

It is not a question of either or, but a question of choice and combinations. Just as you would select the appropriate means of transport to go to different places – you don't take the jumbo jet to go to the local post office, you walk; and you don't drive the car across a lake, you take the boat – you select and combine different media for different purposes according to convenience, functionality and availability.

To successfully exploit the opportunities of today, it helps to acquire an understanding of how media and communication systems have developed in the past. It seems that, when it comes to our history, we always fail the "being-humble-enough" test. Ignorance of history feeds the arrogance of today. We are often too busy and consumed by the new to appreciate the old. But history also tells us time and again that people were wrong to be so quick to dismiss the new. Progress has always depended upon a process of continuous innovation.

Innovation and the rate of change

> Progress, man's distinctive mark alone,
> Not God's, and not the beasts'; God is, they are,
> Man partly is and wholly hopes to be.[9]

Alvin Toffler once pointed out that prior to Gutenberg, only 11 chemical elements were known. The discovery of the twelfth chemical element, antimony, was around the same time as Gutenberg was working on his press. The eleventh chemical element, arsenic, had been discovered two hundred years earlier.

> Had the same rate of discovery continued, we would have by now added two or three additional elements to the periodic table since Gutenberg. Instead, in the 450 years after his time, some seventy elements were discovered. And since 1900 we have been isolating the remaining elements not at a rate of one every two centuries, but of one every three years.[10]

Today, with the power of computer technology and scientific tools, this rate of discovery is accelerating at an even higher pace.

The use of technology has always been a catalyst for social and economic change. Technology is all about creating and mastering tools to enable our progress. But in the past it used to take a lot longer for new technology to find the way to the market-place.

For example, the first patent for a typewriter was issued in England in 1714, but typewriters did not become commercially available until the 1870s. The first patent for a fax machine was issued in 1843 to a British clockmaker called Alexander Bain, who invented a basic prototype for sending images electronically. The first commercial facsimile system was introduced by Abbé Caselli twenty-two years later in 1865 on a line between Paris and Lyon. However, it was not until the 1980s that the fax machine really became a market success. Sales of fax machines exploded in 1986–9 and today the fax is a vital function of every modern office.

Technological innovation is commonly divided into three main phases: invention, exploitation and diffusion. In the case of the typewriter and the fax machine, there was a considerable delay between the first stage (original concept and proven invention), the second stage (exploitation of the idea) and the final stage (market uptake). The cost of this delay, in terms of lost economic and social benefits, can only be speculated upon. It was no doubt a significant loss of opportunity and it is a textbook example of why it is important to manage all three phases of the innovation process in order to reduce time-lag between the various stages of development, so as to achieve success and encourage further innovations.

One technological invention invariably leads to another. Technology feeds on itself. Much effort over the past fifty to sixty years has been devoted to improving technological innovation and what has been termed the innovation loop.

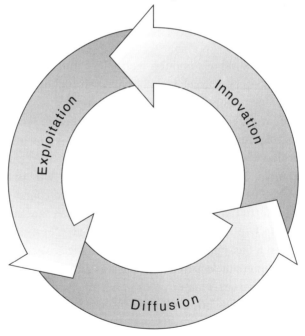

Figure 2   The innovation loop
© A. Leer/Scandinavian University Press, 1996

A good indicator of significant change is when people take the technology for granted and are able to do what they want, without wasting a thought on the technology they are using. The success of communication technology can be measured by ease of use (degree of seamlessness) and the functionality it provides. In other words, technologies that seem invisible to the user are often the ones that have the strongest impact.

Towards the Knowledge Age

Throughout history progress and economic growth have been achieved through intellectual creations and technological innovation. The ability to access information and the knowledge of what the information means have always been fundamental to the progress of humanity.

The traditional approach permits us to carve up our history into periods of time distinguished by certain characteristics. For instance, it is commonly accepted to talk about the evolution of recent history in terms of the Agricultural Age, the Industrial Age and the Information Age. This is no doubt useful in order to explain major events and turning-points in our economic and political history. However, such general labels and distinctions have led many commentators to describe the development of society in terms of distinct and consecutive infrastructures, respectively belonging to each age, rather than one evolving infrastructure. This is misguided, as development of society, and in particular the development of new media and communication technologies, needs to be understood in terms of evolutionary growth, one advance adding to another, not replacing it, as such an approach would imply. There have been shifts of emphasis in the past and there will be further shifts in future as we progress. We no longer place the printing press alone centre stage as the most important vehicle for dissemination of intellectual works. We have added several other essential parts to the infrastructure.

A dictionary definition of "infrastructure" is "an underlying

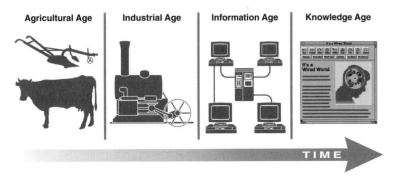

Figure 3 Evolution of infrastructures
© A. Leer/Scandinavian University Press, 1996

foundation" or "the fixed capital equipment in a country",[11] which in society means things such as roads, railways, waterways, power grids, communication systems, factories, schools, universities, hospitals, and so on. During the Agricultural Age the most important part of the infrastructure consisted of farms, animals and ploughs. During the Industrial Age engines and fuels became the central part of the infrastructure.

Today, when we have entered the Information Age, the infrastructure emphasis is on computers and communication networks. As the Information Society advances towards the so-called "Knowledge Age", the infrastructure will evolve to include a growing range of underpinning technologies, software tools and mechanisms, which will enable better use of information, as well as better storage and retrieval.

The little chart in Figure 3 may look neat, but we have to look beyond such very broad-brush definitions and generalisations and search for a more comprehensive understanding of developments. Otherwise, we would be limited to recognising the shape of the wood, but not seeing the trees. We would think we knew how the world operates, but would fail to have any feeling for what life within the forest is really like. We would surf the headlines, rather than study the details. Indeed, most of us have already resorted to this practice, but for a different reason, not to learn how the world works, more as a survival technique for fear of drowning in too much information. Quite a few of us would probably like to see the details, but do not have the time. It is that horrible contemporary disease again – Hastomania fragmentalis information overloadus – spreading like plaque.

Many wise figures and political leaders of the past have pointed out the economic and cultural importance of information and knowledge. From Aristotle, Plato and Caesar to Shakespeare and Adam Smith, all recognised "knowledge itself is power" although it was Francis Bacon (1561–1626) who made this line his.

In more modern Times, T.S. Eliot reflected deeply on the implications of living in an information society:

> Where is the Life we have lost in living?
> Where is the wisdom we have lost in knowledge?
> Where is the knowledge we have lost in information?
>
> ("The Rock", part 1)

So, it would be a mistake to assume that it is only recently, in our time, that information and knowledge has come to play such an important part. That would be an insult to our ancestors. However, in the past the key to economic growth was industrial production. Today, as markets have matured and technology has advanced, it is no longer industrial production that is the most important economic foundation. As the information society develops, the essential economic resource is information and knowledge. This economic shift has caused a substantial value increase in media and information assets. The media and communication industries have consequently become a vital target for investment and concern. The strategic and long-term significance of building the global information society is therefore high on the agenda for both political and commercial players.

Today, it is widely recognised that a prosperous information market is essential in order to gain competitive advantage and achieve continued economic growth. The worldwide market for information technology, products and services is currently valued at US $853 billion, and worldwide investment in telecommunications infrastructure alone is expected to exceed US $200 billion by 2004.[12] The world market for information services is expected to grow from US $275 billion in 1993 to US $465 billion in 1998, an annual growth rate of 11 per cent.[13]

> As we approach the end of the twentieth century, information is a critical force shaping the world's economic system. In the next century, the speed with which information is created, its accessibility, and its myriad uses will cause even more fundamental changes in each nation's economy.[14]
> (US Vice President Al Gore, 1995)

Political leaders play a significant role in facilitating and encouraging the development of the global information society.

> Governments have come to recognise that the telecommunications, information services, and information technology sectors are not only dynamic growth sectors themselves, but are also engines of development and economic growth throughout the economy. With this realisation, governments have sharply focused their public policy debates and initiatives on the capabilities of their underlying information infrastructures. The United States is but one of many countries currently pursuing national initiatives to capture the promise of the Information Revolution.[15]
> (Ronald H. Brown, US Secretary of Commerce, 1995)

The rise of the global information infrastructure (GII)

During the period 1993–6, governments around the world announced plans to develop so-called "national information infrastructures" (NIIs) which were quickly extended to include a "global information infrastructure" (GII).[16] The year 1993 was significant in the history of the GII. Government initiatives in the United States, Europe, Singapore and Japan, sparked off debate world-wide on the use of information and communication technologies, and the implications for economic and social change. These initiatives have become important milestones in the process of building the global information society.

In the United States, President Clinton announced an "Agenda for Action" for the creation of a national information infrastructure. He set up the White House Information Infrastructure Task Force to work with Congress and the private sector to develop comprehensive telecommunications and information policies aimed at articulating and implementing the Administration's vision for the National Information Infrastructure (NII).

In Europe, President Delors of the European Commission presented the *WhitePaper on Growth, Competitiveness and Employment* calling for action to establish a European infrastructure. In response to this paper followed the so-called Bangemann Report, which recommended a course of action towards a European Information Society.

Japan's Ministry of Posts and Telecommunication (MPT) announced the development of "a new information communication structure" and NTT, the main Japanese telecommunication carrier, launched a 25-year programme called "OFL-21" (Optical Fibre Loop for the 21st century), which aims to build a broadband network that will reach every business, school and home by the year 2015.

The US information superhighway: the US NII Agenda for Action and GII Agenda for Co-operation

Clinton and Gore put much of the emphasis of their 1992 presidential campaign, on the importance of building information superhighways and a 21st-century infrastructure. They stressed the importance of developing a national information infrastructure as fundamental to economic growth.[17] Clinton called for a new economic policy that would include an information infrastructure strategy:

> In the new economy, infrastructure means information as well as transportation. More than half the US workforce is employed in information-intensive industries, yet we have no national strategy to create a national information network. Just as the interstate highway system in the 1950s spurred two decades of economic growth, we need a door-to-door fiber optics system by the year 2015 to link every home, every lab, every classroom, every business in America.[18]

Having won the election, President Clinton and Vice President Gore could move on to implement their ideas and make sure that the development of an advanced national information infrastructure (NII) became a top US priority. In September 1993 the Clinton administration launched "The National Information Infrastructure: Agenda for Action".

> A major goal of the NII is to give our citizens access to a broad range of information and information services. Using innovative telecommunications and information technologies, the NII – through a partnership of business, labour, academia, consumers, and all levels of government – will help the United States achieve a broad range of economic and social goals.[19]

The White House set up the Information Infrastructure Task Force (IITF)[20] to "articulate and implement the Administration's vision for the NII". All the key agencies concerned with telecommunication and information policy are represented on the Task Force, which operates under the White House Office of Science and Technology Policy and the National Economic Council. A high-level Advisory Council for the Task Force was also established, to function initially for two years. The Advisory Council consists of a broad range of experts from the private sector, academia, state and local governments, and public interest groups.

The IITF has so far set up three committees with a number of focused working groups:

1 A Telecommunication Policy Committee,[21] which will "formulate a consistent position on key telecommunications issues". The committee has a Working Group on Universal Service, which will "work to ensure that all Americans have access to and can enjoy the benefits of the NII."
2 An Information Policy Committee,[22] which is dealing with "critical information policy issues that must be addressed if the NII is to be fully deployed and utilised". The Committee has three working groups:

A Working Group on Intellectual Property Rights, which is focusing on "protecting copyrights and other IPRs in an electronic world".

A Working Group on Privacy, which is dealing with "Administration policies to protect individual privacy despite the rapid increase in the collection, storage and dissemination of personal data in electronic form".

A Working Group on Government Information, which "focuses on ways to promote dissemination of government data in electronic form".
3 An Applications Committee,[23] which is "co-ordinating the Administration efforts to develop, demonstrate and promote applications in Information Technology in manufacturing, education, healthcare, government services, libraries and other areas". The Committee has a Working Group on Government Information Technology Services (GITS), which co-ordinates "efforts to improve the application of information technology by Federal agencies".

Everyone involved in this work soon realised that it would be impossible to limit the NII to national borders and that the development of the information infrastructure is a global issue of international concern. The Clinton administration responded by extending the plans for the NII to include the global information infrastructure. This was the background for Al Gore's now famous speech at the ITU conference in Buenos Aires in March 1994, where he presented the so-called "US Agenda for Co-operation". There is a copy of this speech in the appendices. This was further elaborated and issued in a press release at the G7 summit meeting in Brussels on 27 February 1995.

Vice President Gore called upon every nation to establish an ambitious agenda to build the GII, using the following five principles as the foundation:

- encouraging private sector investment;
- promoting competition;
- providing open access to the network for all information providers and users;
- creating a flexible regulatory environment that can keep pace with rapid technological and market changes; and
- ensuring universal service.

The purpose of this GII: Agenda for Co-operation is to amplify these five principles and to identify the steps the United States, in concert with other nations, can take to make the vision of the GII a reality. We hope that it will also serve as the basis for engaging other governments in a consultative, constructive, and co-operative process that will ensure the development of the GII for the mutual benefit of all countries.

By interconnecting local, national, regional, and global networks, the GII can increase economic growth, create jobs, and improve infrastructures. Taken as a whole, this world wide "network of networks" will create a global information marketplace, encouraging broad-based social discourse within and among all countries.[24]

The European approach

The US Agenda for Action on the National Information Infrastructure, September 1993 by Vice President Gore and the Clinton administration, provoked a widespread debate also in Europe. In December 1993 the European Council accepted the European Commission's *White Paper on Growth, Competitiveness and Employment*.[25] This proposed an action plan based on five priorities:

- stimulate the use of information technologies, through strategic projects with a European dimension;
- provide basic trans-European services such as ISDN and broadband;
- create an appropriate regulatory framework to address issues such as privacy, security and intellectual property;
- develop training on new technologies; and
- improve industrial and technological performance.

The strategic projects address generic services such as interactive video, access to information and electronic mail, and other priority applications such as teleworking, teletraining, telemedicine and the linking of European administrations.

The investment required for these projects is estimated to be 150 billion ECU over the next ten years. The money is expected to come mainly from the private sector. Financial support from national and community authorities is limited to research and development support, feasibility studies, loan guarantees and interest subsidies.

In underlining the importance of an appropriate regulatory framework, the White Paper indicates five areas for possible action:

- end distortions of competition;
- guarantee a universal service;
- speed up standardisation;
- protect privacy and ensure the security of information and communication systems; and
- extend intellectual property law.

The European Council set up two high-level groups to follow up the acceptance of the White Paper. The first, chaired by Commissioner Christophersen, dealt with the financing possibilities of these networks. The second, chaired by Commissioner Bangemann, formulated a concrete action plan to realise the potential of the global information society in Europe. The Bangemann group analysed potential markets and how a potential infrastructure could work, and identified key issues concerning policy and regulatory frameworks. Both groups presented their reports at the EU summit in Corfu, Greece, at the end of June 1994. There is Chapter 1 of the Bangemann Report in the Appendices.

The Bangemann Report quickly became a source of inspiration and a point of reference for governments and organisations both inside and outside Europe. It pulled people together across public and private sectors and gave them something important to talk about. The Bangemann Report, together with Al Gore's now historic speech in Buenos Aires in March 1994, the US NII Agenda for Action and the GII Agenda for Co-operation that followed, were fundamental political documents that came to play a key role worldwide. These initiatives acted as a great stimulus on both sides of the Atlantic.

Initiatives in Asia

Singapore has been become a textbook example of a high tech success story – how a small nation has exploited information and communication technologies to achieve economic growth, political control and a high degree of automation throughout the public and private sector. The government in Singapore published a report in March 1992 called *Information Technology 2000: A Vision of an Intelligent Island*, which describes how the information infrastructure will be used to turn Singapore into an "Intelligent Island" with a complete information network in place by the year 2000.

In Korea, the development of an information infrastructure is regarded as essential to maintain international competitiveness. There is a three-stage plan in operation which aims to "complete a Super-High-Speed Information Network by the year 2015". This will be a broadband network "capable of transmitting multimedia information, voice, images and data at ultra-high speeds".

Japan has taken a strong lead in promoting the global information society in Asia, working closely with other Asian countries to develop a Pan-Asian Information Infrastructure (AII). The Japanese Ministry of Posts and Telecommunications (MPT) also recognises that the creation of an efficient information infrastructure is a global enterprise and therefore has established communication and collaboration with countries around the world, including the United States and the European Commission.

To the Japanese government the information infrastructure represents a chance to use information and know-how instead of material production in order effectively to solve the problems confronting the country. Japan aims to lay fibre-optic cables to every household in the nation by the year 2015 (the same target date as that set by Clinton administration for the NII in the United States). The optical fibre technology will enable interactive, broadband transmissions of enormous amounts of data. The scale of the information industry will expand and countless new businesses are expected to be created once the optical fibre network is in use. "Assuming that the network is in place by 2010, we estimate that the information-communication industry will represent a 12 trillion dollar market and will have created 2.4 million more jobs."[26]

In 1993 Japan set up major project in the Kansal area, where the objective is to research the technical feasibility and cost-effectiveness of an integrated information-broadcasting network, to find out what applications are needed and to investigate regulatory requirements, including copyright issues. The project has a budget of US $98 million and initially involves the optical fibre cabling of 300 households. More than 100 private-sector companies are participating in the project, from telecommunication carriers, broadcasters and hardware manufacturers to trading companies and banks. Network trials started in 1994.

The MPT expect the development of optical fibre networks and applications, and the multimedia industry, to grow rapidly and they are taking strategic action to facilitate the distribution of software that these businesses will generate.

The developing world

The developing world consists of 77 per cent of the worlds population, 58 per cent of its land area and less than 5 per cent of its gross national product. There are, on average, only about 55 television sets and 28 telephones per thousand persons, concentrated in urban areas, in developing countries.[27] In India, for example, there is less than one computer per thousand persons. There are more telephones in the City of London than there are in the whole of Africa.

The developing world is not homogeneous and there are extreme variations in levels of development, forms of government, receptivity to other cultures, and acceptance of high technology. The infrastructure for delivering information technology, products and services is poor with, for example, problems of power supply, lack of trained personnel, obsolete technology, and equipment unable to cope with extreme weather conditions.

There is also a fear of dependence on technology suppliers and on other countries, and a fear that the information products produced outside their respective cultures may corrupt their own values and traditions and spread dangerous radical ideas. These fears can be a barrier to the acceptance of the latest technologies. However, many leaders in the developing world recognise the advantages of information technologies and understand the need to maintain positive international relations in order to secure access to them.

In the process of developing the global information society, provision must be made for developing countries. Access needs to be made available on a worldwide basis, if there is to be a truly global infrastructure.

> It should not matter whether people are poor, physically disabled, have a low IQ or whatever – IT has the potential to bring benefits to almost everybody. It is crucial for us to include as much of the world as possible in our global interconnected village.[28]

The optimistic view is that the GII will reduce the gap between North and South – between rich and poor, by providing developing countries with GII access and thereby creating new opportunities for economic growth. The optimists also believe that developing countries can leapfrog developments which takeadvantage of the GII, because unlike developed countries they start with a clean slate, without any pre-existing infrastructure. Unlike the developed nations, they do not have to resolve the existing legacy of industrial and legal structures. They can avoid the risk of being delayed, for example, by regulatory frameworks.

The pessimistic view is that the GII will do exactly the opposite and further widen the gap between the wealthy and the poor. Commercial interests in the developed part of the world are expanding into new growth markets as their existing markets reach saturation. The pessimists claim that the rich will dominate the poor and that access to the GII will be restricted to those who can afford it. They fear that the winners to benefit from the GII will be the competitive nations of this world and not the starving ones.

Visions of the global information society

The global information society is like an island that is barely visible on the horizon, still some distance ahead. We can see it from our current standpoint, but only through today's spectacles. Our vision is restricted by our experience of the past and what we know today. The success of our journey will largely depend on the ability to adapt and our willingness to change, to sail into unfamiliar waters. As we sail further towards this island of tomorrow, we discover more and more details and we begin to understand the complexities of the new.

One difficulty with describing the current state of the global information society is that people have different views of the world. It is very hard to get the main operators in the market-place and the policy-makers and regulators in governments to agree and share a common perspective of what the global information society is all about. It gets even more difficult to establish some kind of consensus about expectations of future developments.

History demonstrates that "the future" is a moving target. People's concept of the future changes with experience and exposure to new technologies. The future is never what it used to be. Forecasts of the future rarely stand the test of time and can never be accurate, as decision parameters will and do change. We cannot usefully measure the unknown.

Nevertheless, speculating and planning the future is an important activity. In fact we have the power to shape the future today with decisions and actions we take, both as individuals and organisations. Gazing into that crystal ball, attempting to visualise what the future will bring and what role we will play, is essential in order to move forward. Without any concept of the future, we would not be able to define our objectives and set our course in the right direction. Without any vision of the future we would not be

Figure 4 The political vision of the global information society: a central nervous system for public and private sectors

© A. Leer/Scandinavian University Press, 1996

able to stimulate developments or motivate those who will bring progress and deliver results.

Our visions of the future will drive us in a certain direction and influence the choices we make about where we want to be tomorrow. That is why it is important to examine what the future vision of the global information society is and what expectations will follow.

There seem to be three main visions driving the development of the global information society: the political vision, the commercial vision and the social vision. The predominant political vision of the global information society identifies it as the key to prosperity – that is, to a society that optimises the use of digital technologies to secure growth – through an interconnected world where organisations and individuals live more happily networked ever after.

Figure 5 The commercial vision of the global information society: a global marketplace with electronic shopping malls
© A. Leer/Scandinavian University Press, 1996

The political vision can be referred to as an electronic nervous system for government, education, healthcare, culture and commerce.

The commercial vision of the global information society is as a global marketplace consisting of numerous electronic shopping malls. The dominant players advocating this concept come from the entertainment, communication and information industries. Telecommunication, software, media and electronics companies are all investing heavily in what they see as a new market for their products and services. They will want to charge in a variety of different ways for network access, content and other services. This vision is of the global information society as the ultimate global

Figure 6   The social vision of the global information society: a virtual village green
© A. Leer/Scandinavian University Press, 1996

market-place where all consumers can be reached individually, through their network connections – a marketer's dream come true: sellers of all kinds of goods and services can finally capture us all, they know precisely when we are where, who we are, what we buy and what we do.

There is a third vision of the global information society as a social phenomenon – a virtual village green with open networks for individuals to communicate and share ideas on an informal basis. This vision is strongly held by many Internet users, who will want to preserve the use of Internet as a place to access free information and learn, a place for scientists and academics to exchange and develop knowledge.

These different visions are not mutually exclusive and the development of the global information society should be able to accommodate all three. However, it will be increasingly important to separate the economics of constructing the public and the private sectors of the global information society, including, for instance, the cost of maintaining the social value of Internet and the cost of funding continued access to education and cultural heritage.

Emerging global systems

> Is it a fact . . . that, by means of electricity, the world of matter has become a great nerve, vibrating thousands of miles in a breathless point of time? Rather, the round globe is a vast head, a brain, instinct with intelligence! Or, shall we say, it is itself a thought, nothing but a thought, and no longer the substance which we deemed it!"
>
> Nathaniel Hawthorne, *The House of the Seven Gables.*

Nathaniel Hawthorne's reflections upon the invention of electricity seem to fit even better with the invention of the global information infrastructure (GII) – one wonders what he would have written today. People will perceive the global information society in different ways, use different words and interpret developments according to their respective standpoints and level of understanding. But it is still possible to establish an overview which outlines the base technologies and the application domains that will be the backbone of the global information society.

However, this overview will need continuous revision and is not meant to be taken as either complete or static. One certain maxim of today is that things will change tomorrow. Many assume, but nobody knows in specific terms how, the market and society will evolve. We are moving through a major process of transformation and many of the key parts needed to form the infrastructure and content of the emerging global information society are currently in the mould.

As far as emerging global systems for the GII are concerned, there are four basic architectures: telecommunications (including satellite), cable television, digital television and Internet (including Intercast[29]).

Unfortunately there is a lot of confusion between the Internet and the GII (also popularly referred to as the super information highway). The Internet is part of the evolution, but Internet in its present form is a transitory phenomenon. The value-added content on Internet today will gradually be transferred to other high-performance platforms tomorrow, which will be able to offer the broadband capability of future GIS services.

It is important from both economic and political perspectives to distinguish between Internet as a social phenomenon and the construction of the interconnected global networks that will be the economic backbone of future commerce.

The history of Internet is well covered by other publications.[30] However, it is useful to consider the historic connections in order to understand how Internet is constructed and why Internet may be limited to playing a intermediate role in the construction of the GII.

Internet has existed for 21 years. The father of the Internet is the US Defense Department. The origin of Internet was the need for a closed decentralised communication network, which could facilitate military communication, even after nuclear attacks. The US Defense Department's network, called ARPAnet, was connected to a number of other radio and satellite networks – and Internet was born. The network was specifically designed to require a minimum of information from users. Throughout the 1980s network developers within the academic sector (in the United States, Britain and Scandinavia) developed the Internet concept for use as a communication and information tool for science and research purposes. The National Science Foundation (NSF), a US government agency, commissioned the setting up of NSFNET in the late 1980s. JANET was set up in Britain and UNINETT in Norway. These Internet networks and others that followed were based on the Internet Protocol (IP) and technology developed by ARPAnet.

Today, Internet, as a network of networks, has grown to comprise some 30 million users, over 70 per cent of whom are located in English-speaking countries. One particularly fast-growing

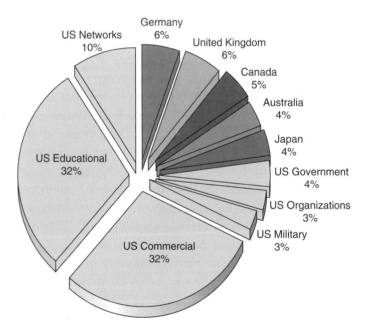

Figure 7 Internet hosts worldwide
Source: Network Wizards

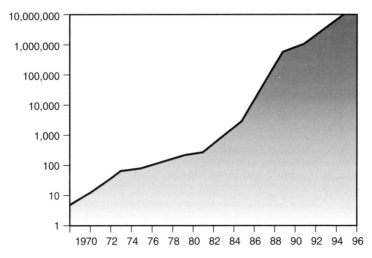

Figure 8 The growth of Internet connections
Source: Network Wizards

segment of the Internet is the World Wide Web (WWW) which has set up its own consortium attracting a range of commercial interests. Estimates vary immensely, but many agree that close to 1 billion people will be connected to Internet by the year 2000.

The Internet is a formation of thousands of interconnecting, open networks. The development of the infrastructure has happened in a bottom-up fashion. It gives individual users the opportunity to "surf" between a myriad of different applications, search for information and use services provided by an increasing number of networks. It also gives individual users the power to interact with others and to become information providers themselves by putting information onto the networks.

There is a sharp contrast between the way in which Internet has been constructed and the way in which the telecommunications, cable and broadcasting networks have been set up in a hierarchical top-down fashion, with massive capital investment.

It is the telecommunications industry that is developing the global broadband network that will provide the essential building-blocks for the GII. The telecommunication industry owns and controls the global fibre optic capacity that has become available in the last decade. It will understandably want to keep control of it in the future and it will want to charge for it. Any computer company, content or service provider or other outfit wanting to capitalise on the GII should not base expansion and development plans on the assumption that access is going to be open and bandwidths free – this may not be the case.

The telecommunication companies are well poised to bankroll the future. Today they derive around 80 per cent of their total revenues worldwide, (around US $600 billion a year), from voice telephony services. However, the voice telephony business is declining. The industry is expecting the decline of voice revenues and portfolio services to continue and it is clearly looking to the GIM and value-added services to generate revenues in future. For instance, Cable & Wireless's forecast shows a very sharp decline in voice revenues: within five years down to 50 per cent, within ten years down to 30 per cent. So, in other words, somewhere between 50 and 70 per cent of the estimated US $3 trillion market in convergence has to come from new entrants, either in competition or in co-operation with the traditional telephone companies.[31]

The cable television networks will also provide a platform for the GII. The industry is currently struggling with high costs of telecommunication lines and satellite television providing the programming. Cable television is limited to physical cable penetration and also suffering from legal constraints, which makes it hard for the industry to move towards GII markets. The cable television industry is clearly conquest territory at the moment for telephone companies as well as other key players set on acquiring a major stake in the GII.

The other interesting development, in terms of global systems, is the emergence of direct satellite television, particularly in the United States. For instance, GM Hughes Networks signed up over 400,000 subscribers within the first nine months.[32] The divisions between current global systems are likely to change or even disappear over the next couple of decades as the digitisation of communication networks continues. Telephony, broadcasting, cable and satellite technologies will eventually come together and gel into the GII of the future.

Intercast is another transitory system using the basic idea of teletext televison services such as Oracle or Ceefax. The data is sent piggybacking (during the VBI) on the standard analogue video signal (NTSC or PAL). Intercast is also broadcasting World Wide Web pages and viewers can in that way have limited access to Internet. However, if the user wants to click on links and use the

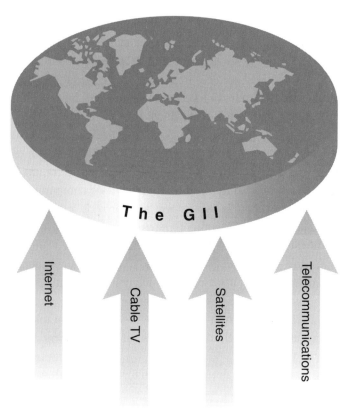

Figure 9 The global information infrastructure
© A. Leer/Scandinavian University Press, 1996

Web in a normal interactive fashion, he or she will need an account with a Internet service provider and a modem.

Intercast was launched on 20 June 1996 and is backed by the Intercast Industry Group (IIG). Companies already providing services include CNN, NBC, WHBG Educational Foundation, Time Warner and QVC shopping channel. Other members of the group so far include Viacom, American OnLine, Intel, Asymetrix, Netscape, Gateway 2000 and Packard Bell.

Intercast is a good example of how the installed base of analogue television sets is being used to gradually introduce new interactive services that will only be fully realised once digital technology and fibre optics have replaced today's analogue systems and coaxial cables. But that will take several years. Digital televison trials are under way and the first commercial digital televison channels are expected in 1997. But the cost of a digital television set will be a major deterrent to uptake in the market: it is currently estimated to be four or five times more than what we pay for our analogue television sets.

We shall see many interim solutions arriving in the market over the next decade which will try to make use of the existing networks and installed platforms, while waiting for this gradual replacement by new fully broadband-capable technology.

Chapter 2
The business challenge

Hype versus reality

Listening to our political leaders deliver their grand visions of the global information society, it is easy to get carried away and be led to believe that this is the all-important answer to "everything" – the stairway to heaven or at least the new world to come.

There is a lot of hype about the global information society generated by political leaders as well as so-called corporate visionaries and "experts" in the field. We are being told that soon every office, every home, every school, every hospital – every individual, every business, every government in the world – will be connected to the GII! There will be instant access to everything from anywhere for everyone via the GII. The GII will be the ultimate one-stop shop. The GII will provide us with entertainment, education, work, health care, financial services, love and friendship and all kinds of information. The GII will penetrate every aspect of society and will bring fundamental change to the way we work and live our lives.

A senior manager at IBM recently told a conference in London to expect TCP/IP Internet connection in their fridges before long. "Wouldn't it be great if the fridge could call you at work or in your car to let you know you were out of milk and tell you to buy some on the way home."[33] Better still, the fridge could call the online home shopping service direct and make sure you never ran out of milk.

I am not sure I feel comfortable with the idea of letting my fridge do my shopping. What if something went wrong here and my fridge ordered a hundred bottles of milk instead of the one I wanted? Would I have to pay? Who would be liable for my fridge's behaviour and shopping activities? Would it be the shop, the network operator, the online shopping service, the network service provider, the retailer who sold me the fridge, the software company that made the programme, the manufacturer of the fridge, the manufacturer of the computer terminal that makes the fridge interactive, my credit card company, my bank – or me? I think I still prefer the milkman, who delivers to my doorstep.

Nicholas Negroponte of the MIT Medialab is excited about what he calls "body area networks" and the idea of "wearable computers": a multipurpose wristwatch which is also a phone, a pager a television, radio and computer, which keeps its computing power in the heel of the shoe! He talks about digital technology being woven into the fabric of our lives, and quite literally too. At a recent national party political conference on "The Challenge of Cyberspace" a British politician announced that "The Internet may well be the biggest thing to happen to mankind since the Creation."[34] GII prophets rave about how we are now about to experience the biggest upheaval since the Industrial Revolution and the GII will have even more impact than the invention of the printing press.

All this hype is then amplified by the media and, of course, by fee-hungry management consultants and by conference organisers. Reports are often biased and media coverage is frequently deliberate and aimed at stirring up excitement to stimulate investment. It is not easy being on the receiving end of all this information, trying to make head or tail of it all. Seeing through the hype in search of the reality is quite a challenge, but of course essential in order to be able to make informed decisions. And although there is a lot to be excited about, many of the expectations created by these promises will probably never be met. That is unfortunate, as it takes a long time to recover from failed expectations. Wrong decisions will no doubt be taken and investments will fail as a result.

It is hard to know when to stop listening to the prophets and corporate gurus. We rely on them to highlight the issues at stake, to provoke our thinking, to bring us new ideas and enthuse us. But we shouldn't let them seduce us. The definition of a guru may be someone who has gone too far and to some extent lost touch with reality.

Gurus are great stimulators, but it is dangerous to rely upon their visions. Beware of the heroes who claim to have the answers. Gurus always simplify the real world to suit their particular ideas which they will not relinquish or willingly change. And change is something we all should be better at. The business model which worked so well yesterday will not necessarily work tomorrow. Always question the gospel preached by the corporate gurus, whether the theme is the "re-engineering revolution", the "learning corporation", "going global", "being digital" or any other fashionable ideas.

Our language is littered with silly metaphors and fashionable buzz-words. We talk of information superhighways, digital revolutions, global access, killer applications, one-stop shopping, tele-working, multimedia "edutainment", and so on. All this playing around with language is symptomatic of a changing society and to some extent we need this tabloid-speak to explore what we do not yet understand. Linguists tell us that when our language changes, behavioural change soon follows.

Many of us feel caught in an avalanche of technological inventions and struggle to understand the impact of change upon individual circumstances – upon business, society and our lives. The sense of being overwhelmed by rapid change and by advances in new technologies makes people give up trying to understand the consequences, let alone keep up to date with developments. Intelligent people resist involvement and withdraw from the cutting edge. Quite often, and understandably, they do so with the attitude that it is futile to invest resources in something which is going to change so quickly anyway.

We all recognise the problem. Should we buy now or wait for

the next, even better, model which is always just around the corner? It is a familiar problem to anybody who has ever considered buying a new car, a computer, a television set, a camera or any other kind of technological invention. Knowing when to invest in what is a major challenge for individual consumers and corporations alike. Will it be all right to purchase an analogue television set or should I wait for the digital sets? Should the company wait for the fibre-optic cable networks or invest in ATM technology?

Those who bought into Philips CD-I (Compact Disc Interactive) technology will have learnt the painful lesson of making an unwise investment. CD-I was a market failure right from the start – and many people tried for years to tell Philips this. This is a classic example of what happens when the perception of the market is completely technology-oriented. It is a story of how a brilliant technology inventor comes to make some fatal misjudgements about the market, because the company refuses to see the limitations of its own "marvellous" invention. Philips tried so hard to create a market for a product that wouldn't last, or would be only short-lived. There was something better around, for instance CD-ROM, multimedia PC software, interactive television and digital video.

The irony is that Philips themselves knew that all along: the company was also busy inventing and developing that better technology, and still is. CD-I was a product that was not wanted or needed by publishers or their customers. Philips made the mistake of embarking on a game they did not have the skills or resources to understand, namely publishing. They strayed away from their core competence and insisted for a very long time that their vision of the CD-I market was real, and not a figment of their imagination. They stopped listening to the market and refused to walk away from a bad investment until it got so bad they had no choice. They had to admit failure and in August 1996 they pulled the curtain down on CD-I. What about those million or so customers who bought CD-I drives and software? Philips will look after them for a while and then they will simply get over it and buy something else exciting and interesting, maybe even from Philips!

There is no escape from digital change. There are only two options, take part or retire. And, assuming we all want to take part, we will not be allowed a lot of thinking time. Seductive marketers are staring us in the face, opportunities keep pounding on our doors, and the pace of events demands action. We live in exciting, complex times. The art of planning and timing one's actions has become all important. Nobody wants to miss the boat and everybody wants to be a winner. As so often in business, timing will be a major factor in determining who the winners will be: "He who seizes the right moment, is the right man" (Goethe's Faust).

Although there are plenty of exaggerated perspectives concerning the meaning of this particular momentum in history, many political and industrial leaders agree that the development of the networked economy is bringing about fundamental and irreversible changes to society. It is a matter of fact that there is considerable commercial and political interest in how to take advantages of the new opportunities of digital technology, multimedia and networked communications. There is a race on between corporations, industrial sectors, countries and governments – each stakeholder investing substantial amounts of energy and resources, hoping to gain competitive advantage by judging the market correctly and picking the right road to success.

How and when the GIs will be realised will depend on four main factors: political action, international co-operation, commercial investment and creative innovation.

The search for a market

But does the "new market" exist? If it does, what is it, where is it and what are the entry options? The global information infrastructure envisaged by Vice President Al Gore in the United States and the global information society (GIS) promoted by President

Santer and Commissioner Bangemann in the European Commission do not yet exist. However, construction is well under way and few will dispute that before long an infrastructure of digital broadband networks will span the globe.

Some will say that the infrastructure is already in place. They are right – in terms of basic technology. Hardware such as network wiring – computers, cables, switches, satellites, and so on, is available. We have at least a multinational, if not a global, infrastructure in place, based upon the existing telecommunications and cable networks, accessible through telephones, television sets and computers. However, substantial developments in technology are still needed to achieve common standards, interoperability between platforms and functional access to open systems.

One thing is certain: there will not be just one broadband network or one type of appliance and interface to connect to the GII. There will be a multitude of interconnected networks and many electronic devices for access and usage. There will be a range of choices for customers – some would say too much choice. The computer industry and the consumer electronics industry are already engaged in fierce competition and will no doubt bombard the market with an ever-growing range of electronic devices and software. In addition to the familiar telephone, television and personal computer, there will be game terminals, network computer terminals, set top boxes, digital video disc players, network radios, infrared remote controls, cellular handsets, pocket computers, smart cards/electronic wallets, and other hand-held devices and products yet to be invented.

It will be exciting to see whether these new products will actually succeed in the market and add some value to customers or whether they will be passing fads and gadgets. Sceptics are warning us that it will all simply lead to electronic overkill. The modern digital gold rush which is driving huge investments in information and media technologies could be deceptive. Is there really a market out there? How will the consumer respond? This is the multi-million-dollar question.

The problem of sizing the market

Organisations across the board are groping in the dark and running into problems when it comes to defining and sizing the market. They are struggling with the identification, the scope and the value assessment of the new market opportunities. It doesn't seem to matter whether you are a dominant player or a new market entrant, the challenge of sizing the market is equally frustrating. Traditional sources and methods of market analysis and forecasting fall short as they are based on the old map of distinct business sectors and cultures. Research methods and market intelligence have been developed differently for a range of industrial sectors which are now converging. Reputable market research companies publish reports that do not take the impact of convergence into account. Consequently, many organisations relying on such sources are basing their strategies on flawed data. Typical market reports are often distorted and quite inaccurate as they distinguish between categories that now overlap, and apply bench-marking figures and industry-by-industry indexes in a manner that no longer makes sense. Important variables are missed out and information is duplicated.

However, this does not stop people using whatever figures they can lay their hands on. It is hard to distinguish between the real and phoney charts. The numerous attempts at estimating what this market will be worth make very amusing reading indeed. There are huge discrepancies between different sets of figures despite the fact that all the reports claim to measure and forecast the same thing and the reports are published by reputable companies. Figures vary, but all the charts seem to have one feature in common – the curve plotting market value rises steeply and consistently upwards, as if it were designed to smell of gold! This is not just an annual US $10–50 billion market, no sir, we are talking hundreds of billions of dollars here. Worldwide estimates of the GIS market range between US $500 billion and US $3 trillion. In the United States alone, people are talking "conservative figures" when they estimate the market to be US $400 billion.

It is interesting to study how analysts arrive at such staggering forecasts. One technique is to base the forecast on accumulated annual expenditure figures from all industrial sectors that can be defined as players in the GIS. Varying estimates of new business to be generated directly from GIS products and services are then added, and the whole is totalled up. This is of course a flawed method, but it is better then some wild guesses, such as those based, for instance, on the entire existing telephony subscriber base instantly being converted to GII subscribers, or all PC owners, or the penetration of CD-ROM drives for that matter. It is better because using actual expenditure figures tells us something about

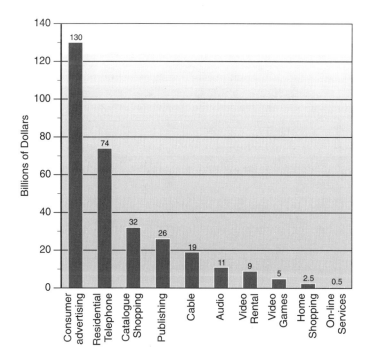

Figure 10 The $300 billion market in converging industries
Source: Gemini Consulting, 1995

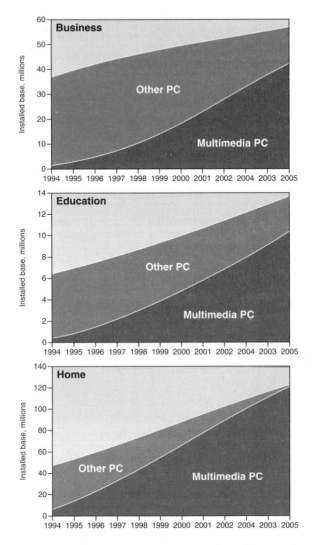

Figure 11a The installed base of PCs and multimedia PCs – business sites (US and Europe) Source: Ovum, 1995

Figure 11b The installed base of PCs and Multimedia PCs – educational establishments (US and Europe) Source: Ovum, 1995

Figure 11c The installed base of PCs and Multimedia PCs – homes (US and Europe) Source: Ovum, 1995

what which customers (where) are willing and able to pay for.

Another technique, which is widely used for sizing the market for publishing products, online services and network traffic, is to base the forecast on the size of the installed base – be it number of Internet host connections, number of telephone or cable subscribers, or the number of PCs and CD-ROM drives shipped, the number of operating software packages sold and so on.

We should be cautious about reading too much into such charts as these. We need to look beyond simplistic summaries of hardware sales and expenditure figures if we want to estimate demands for electronic commerce over GIS networks. Some of the most popular products and services available today have been created without the expectation of a distribution base equal to a share of some installed hardware base or population of network subscribers. A better recipe for success may simply be to go for it, and focus investment on making something the consumer wants.

The fact that most adults have access to a box of matches does not prove there is a market for cigarettes. The tobacco industry relies on far more sophisticated methods for managing market demand for cigarettes and sizing up the market. Investments are based upon psychological knowledge of consumer behaviour as well as tangible facts and hard figures. Demographic data, consumer group surveys, detailed analysis of what attracts people to smoke and why they continue, are all important tools in this process. The health risks linked to tobacco, people's attitudes to smoking, the impact of regulatory frameworks, such as legal constraints with regard to advertising and liability risks, are also significant factors that are taken into account.

The penetration of so-called multimedia PCs is interesting if you happen to be manufacturing or retailing PCs, CD-ROM drives, sound cards or other components for such multimedia PCs. It is also of interest to those who have already produced software programs for this particular platform. But for all others, the penetration of a particular consumer appliance should be of less interest. Although, it is important to know that there is an installed base of x number of y systems out there, it would be wrong to automatically translate this into a market for GIS products and services. The critical factor that will determine the success of a new product or service is not the technology it will run on, but the functionality and attractiveness it can offer the individual consumer. When it comes to electronic devices, computer software and the media industry, consumers are used to rapid change and increasing choice. People will quickly discard the useless and change over if something better comes along.

When organisations are considering which platform to build products and services around, and when consumers are considering what to buy, the critical question should be whether that particular technology can do the job. Ask yourself, is it good enough? Will it serve your purpose and for how long? And don't ask whether this is the ultimate solution – there will always seem to be something better in the pipeline. You'll never get started if you don't take the first step.

Technology is only a small part of what is needed in order to deliver the promises of the global information society. The challenge really begins with the task of understanding how people and organisations will want to use the technology. What kind of products and services will add value and be of interest to the market? Who are the customers and where is the market? This line of questioning leads us into the post-technology stage, where we will have to focus on understanding the user and the content, rather than the container and the context. The user is the one who will ultimately pass judgement on the value of being connected to the GII and who should be directing the show. The user does not care about technology. The nuts and bolts should be invisible to the user. The user should not have to care about whether it is the PC, network terminal, television, telephone or other device that is used for access to the GII. The user is not interested in technology. The user is interested in the content and how the content meets his or her expectations and requirements.

Content is a much more difficult and resource-intensive part of

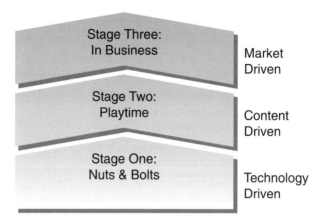

Figure 12 Three main phases in the process of constructing the global information market
© A. Leer/Scandinavian University Press, 1996

the GII construction process than technology is. We have only just begun to play with the new opportunities. The best is yet to come. It was Ernest Hemingway who once said, "A great story is like an iceberg. One-eighth is above the surface; the other seven-eighths is below." Today we are looking at the very tip of the iceberg, mostly ignorant of what lies underneath and beyond the physical infrastructure of the wired world. Most investments have so far been driven by technology and the need to control and manage the nuts and bolts. Many organisations are moving rapidly into the next stage driven by the need for content. Together with early adopters in the market they are busy experimenting and playing around with content in many shapes and forms. This activity will not only provide greater knowledge of what new applications can offer, but hopefully also result in better understanding of what the market really wants. It is when this avalanche of early experiments matures into a number of sustainable products and services driven by market demand that organisations reach the third stage and we can call it real business. Innovation will always continue and people will have to make up their minds and place their bets as new achievements are announced and new products emerge. Organisations will continue to invest and more players will enter the market. And inevitably, there will be several shake-outs reducing the number of players and the noise in the market-place. There will be expensive lessons and lost bets, but there will also be exciting results and plenty of winners.

The British film-maker Sir David Puttnam has pointed out that "the CD-ROMs now on the market are digital equivalents of those rather aimless, almost embarrassing, flickering silent movies from before the First World War."[35] We have a long way to go before we realise the potential of a connected society, which, to a large extent, will depend on the ability to identify customer demand and deliver useful content. Few will claim to have reached the third stage yet. Many are between the first and the second stage, looking to content as the critical issue. The US GII Agenda for Co-operation points out:

> The GII extends beyond hardware and software; it is also a system of applications, activities, and relationships. There is the information itself, whatever its purpose or form, e.g., video programming, scientific or business databases, images, sound recordings, library archives, or other media. There are also standards, interfaces, and transmission codes that facilitate interoperability between networks and ensure the privacy and security of the information carried over them, as well as the security and reliability of the networks themselves. Most importantly, the GII includes the people involved in the creation and use of information, development of applications and services, construction of the facilities, and training necessary to realise the potential of the GII. These individuals are primarily in the private sector, and include vendors, operators, service providers, and users.

The Content Race

We are standing at the very start of the 'Content Race' – today's equivalent of the great Gold Rush – and many hopeful would-be GII players have become serious content gamblers. There is a growing sense of panic among those who have invested the most in the technology as they realise that technology alone is useless – the GII needs content. "Content" is another buzz-word. Many prominent speakers at business conferences around the world frequently proclaim "Content is King!" and the audience applaud, recognising that the mere physical shape of the GII leaves little to be excited about. We need something to fill our magic box with. At the turn of the century, many of us will have access to an estimated 500 television channels. What are we going to fill them up with? The lyrics from that Bruce Springsteen song come to mind: ". . . fifty channels on the TV and nothing on".

Content may be the life-blood of the GII, but unlike human blood there isn't a universal type O suitable for all. There is no type-O donor among the content owners, capable of pumping out generic content acceptable across the GII. The fact that the term "content" is being used as a blanket label for some omnipotential bag of magic demonstrates a lack of understanding for what content means related to the needs of specific user-groups connected to the GII. Content only becomes meaningful the moment an individual customer makes use of it.

It was the technology-oriented players – the telecommunication and software industry – who started using the term "content" some time in 1993–4, and unfortunately it seems to have stuck. Authors, publishers and producers now find themselves renamed as "content providers" and government officials talk about "the content industries". Now there is a pressing need for differentiation between different kinds of content and refinement of activities, products and services within the GII. We suffer from the fact that the development of the global information society originates from technology. Consequently we have inherited an outlook that is coloured by technical capability, rather than commercial and social benefits. We need to shift our perspective in such a way that we can focus clearly on the main driver of this development. It is not the content that is King, but the customer. We should have customers placed at the centre of our focus, not technology. It is customers and market demand that will drive the development of this market.

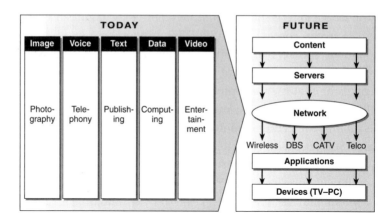

Figure 13 A technology-oriented view of the market
   Source: Jagdish Sheth, Emory University

Who the customer is will, of course, depend on what type of business you represent and what you have to offer. There is a lot of confusion regarding markets, caused by the notion and developments of the GII. Many organisations are suffering from a serious state of identity crisis. It is a classic problem – how to grow and prosper beyond your current status. We often forget who we are when we let ourselves be seduced by prospects which we cannot

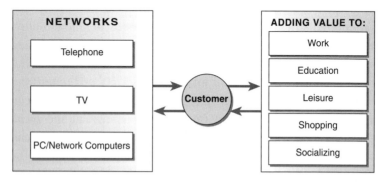

Figure 14 A customer-oriented view of the market
   © A. Leer/Scandinavian University Press, 1996

attain. Success in one area often makes organisations over-confident and arrogant. Just because a company has been immensely successful as a telephony provider, it does not follow that they can replicate this success in the business of broadcasting or publishing. Companies frequently forget who they are and what their competitive advantage is. They lose sight of what their core competencies are and neglect their own assets in an attempt to capitalise on what they do not yet control, or even comprehend. They embark on over-ambitious and omni-potential growth strategies, which bring more failures than success.

The challenge of exploiting the business opportunities of the GIS is that no one company can do it alone. We need to collaborate and reach outside our own comfort zone and core expertise. Even the richest and most dominant players, such as, for instance, the telecommunication giants or media/software companies like Time Warner, Microsoft, the BBC or Bertelsmann, will have to let go of the degree of control they have enjoyed in the past and enter into a multitude of collaborations and strategic partnerships to enable them to deliver products and services within the GII.

The meaning of convergence

The concept of convergence is frequently used to describe the development of the global information society. Unfortunately, the term is often applied carelessly as a crude blanket label, often giving people a false impression that the entire world is about to converge into One – one technology, one market, one business, one type of customer, one form of government, one model for education, and so on. That is of course not the case, and we need to pay a lot more attention to precisely what the so-called process of convergence means.

Convergence is taking place in a number of areas at various levels; in science and technology, in industrial sectors, in the marketplace, in the legal and regulatory domain, in education and research, and in politics. We need to distinguish between these different areas of convergence in order to see how they interrelate and to understand the changes taking place around us. The process of convergence started with previously separate technologies coming closer together as a direct consequence of the advances made in microchip and computer technology. The most profound changes will probably take place as a result of the process of technological convergence of the previously separate telecommunications, cable, information, publishing and mass media industries. These industrial sectors are now often referred to as "the converging industries". Borders that once separated them are increasingly being blurred. In the past we had different types of networks for the delivery of mail, print, telephony, radio, television and data services. These networks are regulated differently and usually by separate authorities. In a digital world, these services can be combined and offered over the same transmission and delivery system. In the words of the US GII Agenda for Co-operation:

> Multiple networks composed of different transmission media, such as fiber optic cable, coaxial cable, satellites, radio, and copper wire, will carry a broad range of telecommunications and information services and information technology applications into homes, businesses, schools, and

Company	Multimedia Content	Multimedia Distribution	Hardware/ Electronics	Software	Telecom.
Microsoft	X	X	X	X	X
BBC	X	X		X	
AT&T	X	X	X	X	X
IBM		X	X	X	
Pearson	X	X		X	
Bertelsmann	X	X	X	X	X
Time Warner	X	X	X	X	X
BT	X	X	X	X	X
ICL	X	X	X	X	
Kirch Group	X	X	X	X	X
Viacom	X	X	X	X	X

Figure 15 Examples of cross-industry convergence in the market
© A. Leer/Scandinavian University Press, 1996

hospitals. These networks will form the basis of evolving national and global information infrastructures, in turn creating a seamless web uniting the world in the emergent Information Age. The result will be a new information marketplace, providing opportunities and challenges for individuals, industry, and governments.

The Strategic Alliance Syndrome

The current scenario is dominated by players from traditionally separate industries, each providing its independent infrastructure, be it telephony, broadcasting, cable television, online business information, publishing, or others. These key players are planning for a future where these infrastructures will merge or interconnect. The expectation is that the separate means of communication will be integrated in digital services to be provided throughout society. Stakeholders involved are consequently investing in developing new applications which can take advantage of the new GII services.

As a result, companies realise that if they are to respond to this market development, they will need resources and skills outside their traditional domain. Consequently, all the key commercial players who are busy shaping the GII have reached outside their own entity to form relationships with others in combined efforts to create products and services for the global information market.

The convergence of technologies is causing fundamental change to the structure of traditional industries. New business models require new market positions. Collaboration across industrial and cultural borders is required to succeed in the new environment. The strategic response of many companies is one of growth through acquisitions and/or strategic alliances as part of a process of vertical or horizontal integration.

This growing trend of strategic alliances forming in the market has been going on since the early 1980s. However, in the past, strategic alliances have usually been limited to two-company alliances, that is, joint ventures. Today, we see groups of companies establishing formal links with each other. There is an increasing trend for industrial sectors to merge activities and build collaborations across a wide spectrum of skills and resources. Software, computer, and consumer electronics companies, telecommunication and cable operators, network service providers, broadcasters, publishers, chip manufacturers, banks, distributors and retailers, are all forming alliance groups in order to develop new products and services.

> A new form of competition is spreading across global markets: group versus group. Call them networks, clusters, constellations, or virtual corporations, these groups consist of companies joined together in a larger overarching relationship.[36]

The new evolving market structure

The growth of strategic alliances and the degree of vertical and horizontal integration in the market-place have fundamentally changed the structure of the market. It no longer makes sense to apply the traditional distinctions between industrial sectors. Telecommunication carriers are now also broadcasters, cable oper-

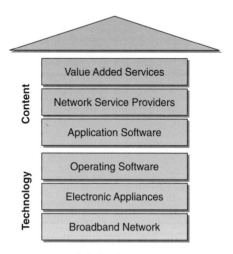

Figure 16 The emerging global information market structure
© A. Leer/Scandinavian University Press, 1996

ators are telephony providers, film companies are generating more revenue from selling merchandise than they do from films, libraries have become publishers, software developers are offering banking services, consumer electronics companies are running film studios and publishing all kinds of media content, and so on.

The emerging market structure can be split up into six layers representing the key business areas or reshuffled industrial sectors:

Layer 1.   Broadband Network
Telephony, satellite, cable and broadcasting companies owning and developing the physical communication network. Companies manufacturing microchips, security technology and network control systems will provide the "engine power", the security and quality control systems needed to operate the network. Standards organisations and industry regulators will ensure that standards and regulations are followed.

Layer 2.   Electronic appliances and components
Companies providing consumer electronics, PCs, hardware-based user interfaces (from smart cards to set top boxes).

Layer 3.   Operating software
Computer and software companies providing network and PC operating systems.

Layer 4.   Application software
Companies developing and publishing computer programmes to make the various applications work, including user interfaces.

Layer 5.   Network service providers
Companies providing network access to a range of facilities such as Internet, interactive television, cable and satellite.

Layer 6.   Value-added information services
Government administrations and public services, including

education and national health. Companies providing online services within various sectors, for instance:

- Banking and financial services
- Healthcare
- Business and professional
- Academic and scientific research
- Libraries and archives
- Education
- Mass media
- Entertainment and culture
- Home shopping.

And companies offering support services:

- Advertising and marketing agencies
- Consultancy.

Key players in the market-place are searching for optimum business models, busy trying to pick the winning positioning combination in this market structure. Many of them are moving up towards the value-added services. Take the telecommunication companies: all the larger once have expanded into new products and services, growing out from their home base in the technology domain right through to the top layer in the content domain.

Redefining the market

Most organisations will have to redefine their markets. Market dynamics are changing and the market can no longer be reached efficiently through the traditional way of segmenting it. Boundaries between once very different markets are getting increasingly blurred. There is a process of convergence going on that makes it necessary for many companies to review their marketing strategies. The old map of the market does not reflect the changed land-

THE BUSINESS CHALLENGE 63

Figure 17 A traditional way of segmenting the market
© A. Leer/Scandinavian University Press, 1996

scape. By investigating the degree of change and redrawing the map according to the findings, companies find a world of new marketing challenges and opportunities. Old, outdated market definitions are thrown away. New ways of re-segmenting the market are applied, which has enormous implications for the organisational structure of companies and for how they manage their operations. Many companies find they have to reorganise themselves completely in order to operate competitively and match the changing landscape of the market.

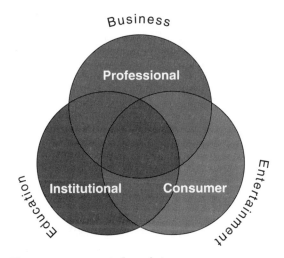

Figure 18 The new re-segmented market
© A. Leer/Scandinavian University Press, 1996

Challenges and strategic responses of key players

The key players in the development of the global information society come from both public and private sectors.

The public sector

Many governments see the global information society as an opportunity for social, cultural and economic reform. Information networks offer many new opportunities to rationalise public sector activities and operate public services more efficiently. The establishment of an information infrastructure can also add value to the quality of the welfare state by offering new means of delivering education, providing health-care services and stimulating cultural activities. Governments and their administrations play an important role in setting policies and determining regulatory frameworks. As we have seen with recent political campaigns, many of them actively pursue an agenda of building a global information society, launching initiatives aimed at stimulating private investment and facilitating growth in the information market.

There is a general economic climate and a political attitude throughout the competitive world, which favours the freedom of market forces and a transfer of public ownership and responsibilities to the private sector. This is manifesting itself in a number of ways, most notably by the increasing number of public companies being privatised and by the deregulation of industrial sectors. The predominant political and economic conviction sees the building of open competitive markets and the commercial enterprise as the key to efficiency and economic growth.

However, there are several sectors of the global information society which will never be able to operate accordinag only to commercial rules, for instance, health, education, culture and scientific research. These will continue to need public funding and support. They will remain a primary concern and responsibility for democratic governments and public organisations. Education has moved to the top of the political agenda. This is a direct consequence of the shift towards a new networked economy where the key resource is information and knowledge. Economic growth now depends on the intellectual capacity of a skilled workforce.

The escalating growth of information and knowledge have put enormous pressures on the funding of education and research. Libraries, archives and museums are also struggling with a severe mismatch between given mandates and available funds.

Information technology has wrought sweeping changes across society, affecting most professions and functions. The need for learning new skills and for acquiring new knowledge is predominant. It is no longer sufficient to limit the individual's time in education to childhood and youth. The traditional formal education provided by schools and universities is not enough. The need for retraining and continuous access to education has boosted development of the concept of lifelong learning.

Ironically, the same information technology that has put so much pressure on the educational system is also proposing solutions and ways of meeting the crisis and improving the capacity of the system. Global networks and access to vast knowledge stores are creating exciting opportunities for delivering educational products and services in new ways. There is an explosion in distance learning experiments, of which many are funded by the private sector, in addition to those funded by the public sector.

Education is receiving a lot of commercial interest and this is something new. The private sector's new-found love for education is driven by the perception of a great market opportunity. Their involvement brings much-needed investment in the educational sector. However, not everybody is comfortable with this. As the European Commissioner of Education, Madame Cresson, once said, pointedly reminding her audience, "Business people are no angels!"[37]

Sir David Puttnam is one businessman and film-maker who early recognised what he calls the convergence between education, business and entertainment. He launched the idea of creating an "Education Hollywood" in Britain, capitalising on the country's main export asset – the English language – and its considerable experience and skill in publishing educational materials. He has attracted support and involvement from a number of organisations in both the public and the private sector. Together with the British Council, the BBC, the Open University and others, he is working on developing a World Learning Network.

Both public and private sectors recognise the value of education and its critical role as a catalyst for a healthy networked economy. The quality and success of education will be fundamental to how the global information society develops: "Well-educated, well-trained, highly motivated and creative people... These are the best assets for Europe to live and prosper in the digital world of the next millennium."

But there is no doubt that there is much confusion and frustration about what the interface between private and public sectors should be, in particular as regards the future operation of educational systems, libraries and other cultural institutions. In many countries there is heated debate over roles and responsibilities. How far does public responsibility extend? How much should the private sector take charge of? Who will pay for the custody of and access to the world's growing knowledge stores? Who will pay for the continued creation of new knowledge?

The taxpayer alone will not be able to foot the bill. The market will only pay for what it favours or is commercially viable. There is a desperate need for new funding models for education, research and culture. Policy-makers are busy searching for solutions and looking at what can be achieved by collaborative effort between the public and private sectors. However, the details of what will be shared-responsibility models remain mostly in the dark and will no doubt be the subject of much debate.

The educational sector will probably alleviate some of the economic pressures by getting more involvement and support from the private sector. Private enterprise is excited about the scores of identifiable consumers in this sector and the promise of new potential buyers of educational products and services. But the library system, as we have defined it in terms of roles and responsibilities, will have great difficulty operating without considerable public and non-profit funding.

Many of the library services can be successfully privatised and have been in several countries, most notably in the United States and in Britain. But today's market forces do not consider the needs of future generations. What our great-grandchildren may want to have simply does not feature in our current commercial equations.

The role of the libraries as the appointed custodians of our cultural heritage is widely accepted, but not often enough applauded. Libraries across the world should be recognised for what they do and the kind of challenges they face in their struggles to cope with exponential information growth. This sector needs much more involvement from governments and from the private sector and individuals who can help solve the crisis of the world's growing information mountains.

Paper alone can no longer carry the volumes of published knowledge. The world now depends upon information technology to provide the means to handle the growing literature, cultural heritage, and scientific and scholarly information, and to achieve effective methods for storage, distribution and retrieval. This effectively means substantial investment in digital technology and a complete overhaul of library operations.

Libraries have come a long way since the first library was founded in 1250 BC by King Ramses II of Egypt with a stock of 20,000 papyrus scrolls. The more famous library of Alexandria was founded during the early part of the 3rd century BC with a collection of 200,000 scrolls of papyrus and linen. Today the largest library in the world is the US Library of Congress. By the end of 1994 it had a collection of over 28 million books in 470 languages and a digital store of 35 information databases with access to over 26 million records. The library's databases have around 20 million users located in 100 countries around the world. In Europe the largest national library is the British Library with over 18 million books.

Library policies vary from country to country. For instance, electronic storage and distribution of works subject to copyright are permitted in the United States subject to certain restrictions and conditional requirements, but in most European countries it would be illegal for libraries to do so. Many libraries have not yet got the digital mandates they need in order to maintain their traditional roles and to continue to provide an adequate service level to their users.

The problem of incompatible national library policies and systems causes problems and friction on an international level. The digital networks of the global information society operate across national borders. It does not matter which country you are in – you can always log into the information databases of, for instance, the Library of Congress or the British Library, and download the information you need. So which national jurisdiction applies? The library cannot control through which jurisdictions the information is transmitted or which network connections are used for each of the millions of electronic requests they receive. Library policies and systems need to be harmonised across the world and standard solutions need to be resolved on a multinational level.

This is a contentious political issue as it stirs up national feelings about the right to determine the nation's cultural policy irrespective of what other nations do. National control over internal affairs is a well-established principle and not many politicians would dare to rock that boat. But times are changing and the new networked economy disregards national borders. Membership of the networked economy and the global information society is going to be far more important than national citizenship and the country of origin.

Power will not be in the hands of the nation state, but in the digital hands of a wired world.

The private sector

For the private sector the wired world represents a massive opportunity for business development and economic growth. It is primarily global electronic commerce and the potential of access to large numbers of networked users that attract companies to the digital market-place. Digital networks have facilitated the development of electronic shopping malls where masses of content is supplied, including both tangible and intangible goods and services. Navigation tools, standards and protocols allow consumers to find and purchase the information, products and services they want. Sales of goods and services through the Internet was worth an estimated US $300 million in 1995 and is expected to escalate over the next few years.

By July 1996, 70 per cent of the Fortune 100 companies had established their own Web site on Internet. The majority of them are primarily using the World Wide Web (WWW) for public relations and marketing purposes. But as more Internet networks can offer companies a sufficient degree of network security, a growing number of companies are also trading goods and services online.

Information and media assets will increasingly account for the most significant volume of transactions over global networks. Consequently it is the so-called content industries that have moved centre-stage on the economic agenda. Apart from education and culture, we also need to count the information and media industries as the most critical assets in a knowledge-based economy.

The changing world of advertising

The information and media industries rely heavily on advertising revenues. Any significant shifts in advertising spending figures will have an immediate impact on cashflows and levels of media output. How advertisers chose to spend their advertising dollars will be a main driver in the shaping of the global information market. It will be critical for publishers, broadcasters, network operators and information service providers to find ways of capturing and holding on to their shares of the advertising market.

There will be significant changes in media advertising as this market develops. It may not worry the media industry so much today, as advertising spending patterns have yet to absorb the new forms of advertising. Most advertisers still define advertising that uses new media channels as a research activity. But this is rapidly changing as the new media channels mature and work out their business models.

Advertising rates on Internet are in many cases based on a combination of a monthly fixed charge and a charge for the number of actual "hits", that is, the number of times (or number of users by whom) the advertisement is accessed. Rates vary tremendously. Some offer space for between US $10,000 to 30,000 per month or US $15,000–18,000 per 1 million "hits".

The new wired world of connected consumers brings many new opportunities for advertising. Advertising agencies and their clients are busy experimenting with new methods and new channels for advertising. Traditionally, media advertising has been split into five main revenue streams: magazines, newspapers, radio, television and film. Now there are many more to consider: cable networks, online information networks, online banking, interactive television, digital radio, multimedia games, and the phenomenal growth of Internet and WWW with all its networks and different applications.

The competition for advertising revenue will be fierce as the information market continues to expand. Advertisers will bask in a world full of advertising space and thrive in a buyer's market. The advertising choices they make determine the funding of the media and will eventually make the fat lady sing. Allocation of advertising spending dollars will drive the process of convergence and market concentration even further, as many players in the global information market will have to join forces to be able to demonstrate a market reach attractive enough to advertisers.

The networked market is also changing the style and presentation of advertising. Never before in our history have advertisers had so much information about their markets and access to so many tools to accumulate knowledge about their individual customers. Market intelligence has never been as intelligent as it is today. Advertisers can make use of sophisticated customer profiles enabling them to target customers with very specific advertising tailored to individual interests, tastes and buying power. This is called personalised advertising.

Network advertising also means exciting possibilities for interaction between advertisers and customers. This in turn means new opportunities for developing customer relationships. Closer communication with customers can only be a good thing for advertisers. Feedback and input from customers will improve the ability to deliver competitive products. Advertisers will learn more' about customers and customers will learn more about what the advertisers have to offer, and thus be able to make more informed purchasing decisions.

Direct marketing over networks can be convenient for customers, especially if it is integrated with features such as automated ordering facilities, secure payment and delivery on demand. Direct marketing can also be more profitable for companies, as the cost of sale is reduced and intermediaries can be removed from the equation. But direct marketing also puts new pressure on companies, which will have to make decisions about how to organise their marketing operation. A growing number of organisations are developing their own direct marketing systems, including direct mail order. Many chose to out-source the direct marketing operations and make use of the broad range of advertising and marketing services available.

Another interesting development is the upsurge in "collaborative advertising", in which companies from different sectors collaborate on joint advertising schemes and/or enter into partnerships in order to combine their products and services in new ways. In the past it was unthinkable to associate certain products with others. But today it seems only natural to bundle disparate products together to promote particular images. For instance, who would have thought that it could make sense to bundle subscriptions to the *British Medical Journal* with classic cars, good wine selections and holidays abroad. Once that threshold is crossed, it pushes back the frontiers of advertising and opens endless new opportunities for advertising products and services in different ways.

Network advertising can be integrated with the actual product or service in entirely new ways. A television soap opera, can for instance, be built around a series of products that feature in the programme. And advertisers can use all kinds of programming to create interactive services – even sports and news. Viewers can select and order products they see in the programmes; be it that bikini worn by Pamela Anderson of Baywatch or those trainers worn by Linford Christie, that pink shirt of Prime Minister John Major, or perhaps that hat selection of her Majesty the Queen of England will appeal.

"Interactive" advertising is changing the focus of advertising from individual product-pushing to concept-building. Advertisers increasingly seek to understand the individual circumstances of customers and their needs and wants. They are selling products and services with a view to supporting certain lifestyles and/or work styles.

The evolution of new types of advertising also means that advertising agencies will have to develop new skills and ways of working with clients. Clients will need to be much more involved in the design and process of advertising. The relationship between the client and the advertising agency will change as a result and they will have to come much closer to each other's business.

The concept of the customer receiving only the advertising to which he or she is susceptible, is attractive to both customer and advertiser. But this development can also have implications for individuals' right to privacy as it presupposes the detailed recording and usage of personal information. It also raises concern over media ethics, advertising standards and consumers' rights of protection. The risk of potential abuse of new forms of powerful advertising will no doubt be on the political agenda very soon, if it is not there already. There is already considerable unease in the regulatory camps dealing with laws of advertising, privacy, consumer rights and the media. It will be a real challenge to redefine the regulatory framework in such a way that it will stimulate the economic growth of the global information market, while safeguarding the principles of media regulation and advertising standards, which have delivered the quality and richness of the media content we have available today.

The changing world of publishing

This is an exciting time to be a publisher. Here the terms "publisher" and "publishing" refer not only to the world of print, but to all kinds of publishing products, including software programmes, photographs, artwork, music, radio and television programmes and film. The proliferation of new distribution channels has created tremendous opportunities for publishers to expand their markets. The hunger for content – this seemingly endless appetite for "stuff" to fill up the networks – is a great challenge for those publishers who know how to embrace change and manage new channel structures.

Media content, more precisely "publishing products", are rapidly growing in their value share of nations' Gross National Product. However, if we were to set up a worldwide, country-by-country table of media output it would not paint a picture of equality. The dominance of the American media industry is staggering. Europe and the rest of the world should applaud US achievements in the media, rather than moan about Americanisation and the US invasion of national cultures. Governments and enterprises need to recognise why their own countries have not been able to match the success of the United States in this respect and they need to come up with constructive strategies to make their media industries more competitive.

Other national media industries have not enjoyed the same

Figure 19 Oh baby, fill up my band-width
© A. Leer/Scandinavian University Press, 1996

prosperity and support as their US counterparts. The decline of the excellent British film industry is a rather sad story of how a potentially very media rich nation was unable to grow and stay competitive and how it was eventually overshadowed by the United States. Many valuable British media assets were enticed abroad and quite a few bought for a penny by US investors. It is a prime example of intellectual and cultural drain on a nation's competitive resources. The question for Britain, and indeed for other nations, now is whether that lesson has been learnt or whether the same thing will be allowed to happen all over again with the digital media.

The British film-maker Sir David Puttnam has pointed out that the United States was the only nation to take the film industry really seriously from the start, in spite of the fact that Europe invented the cinema, developed it and even exported in to the United States:

> It was President Wilson who recognised, as early as 1917, that where American movies went, American goods and influence would soon follow. He put it in this terms: 'The film has come to rank as the very highest medium for the dissemination of America's plans and America's purposes.' Every US President since has upheld that view and ensured that a legislative and regulatory regime was produced to match it. It goes some considerable way towards explaining why America has so completely dominated the history of cinema, and continues to do so today.[38]

Film and television programmes have become the biggest export asset of the United States. Of course this has huge cultural impact on the global information market and on individual countries. It raises serious questions about the competitiveness of other nations. It also begs the question of what will happen to national identity, to language and different cultures around the world.

We certainly do not want a world of only one identity, one language and one type of culture. And we must make sure that all

Language	1992		1993		1994		1995		1996	
English	1,489	67%	2,554	71%	3,921	73%	5,038	71%	9,317	72%
German	182	8%	283	7%	451	8%	735	10%	1,677	13%
French	210	9%	290	8%	445	8%	614	9%	914	7%
Spanish	103	5%	202	6%	326	6%	480	7%	652	5%
Italian	122	6%	173	5%	249	5%	365	5%	545	4%
Japanese	128	6%	213	6%	309	6%	282	4%	391	3%
Dutch	83	4%	115	3%	148	3%	148	2%	227	2%
Swedish	22	1%	26	1%	34	1%	38	1%	68	1%
Russian	2	0%	3	0%	8	0%	15	0%	64	0%
Danish	16	1%	28	1%	33	1%	32	0%	42	0%
Total	2,213		3,597		5,382		7,075		12,909	

Many discs contain information in more than one language

Figure 20 CD-ROM and multimedia CD titles by language(s) of discs 1992–1996. Source: TFPL

Area	1993		1994		1995		1996	
Americas	2,273	63%	3,299	61%	4,137	58%	7,323	56%
Europe	1,024	25%	1,583	29%	2,636	37%	5,106	39%
Asia	223	6%	341	6%	317	4%	420	3%
Australasia	79	2%	99	2%	88	1%	122	1%
Middle East	25	1%	13	<1%	12	<1%	59	<1%
Africa	4	<1%	6	<1%	14	<1%	20	<1%

Figure 21 Origins of CD-ROM and multimedia titles 1993-1996
Source: TFPL

that 'stuff' filling up the bandwidth and content spewing out of that "digital hose" is not all American stuff or for that matter all delivered through the English language. The fact is that at the moment 70 per cent of all Internet connections are in the English-speaking world and the United States is clearly driving the bulk of the investment activities in the market.

It should not be difficult to see why it is urgent and of paramount importance for other nations and their individual enterprises to get involved in the global information market. The European Commission is acutely aware of the need for Europe to invest and be in the driving seat. They have launched a number of initiatives designed to improve European competitiveness, drawing upon the strength of individual national cultures and intellectual creativity. But that it is not enough. Every government, every organisation, every enterprise and every individual needs to come to the digital party and figure out their particular way of taking advantage of the opportunities available.

Publishers are getting used to having to operate in a climate of major change induced by digital technology. At first, information technology simply came in the back door. Slowly but surely new tools were introduced and within a few years entire production systems had been completely revolutionised. Typesetters were made redundant and printing works closed down. The old cut-and-paste editing tables and the slow analogue editing techniques in film and television disappeared as computer-based editing systems took over.

Now information technology is revolutionising publishers' markets. And technology know-how can no longer remain the domain of just the IT and production departments. All the management functions and all the creative, the marketing and distribution resources need to learn. All the managers need to take those digital lessons and acquire the technology know-how and why and how much and when.

Publishers are experiencing a kaleidoscope of emerging new business opportunities, driven by new market demands for publishing products. Traditional roles are changing, industries are converging, markets are being deregulated and globalised.

Technological progress has made it possible to disseminate and manage information in new ways. Electronic mixed-media publishing, digital libraries, distance learning, teleworking and online shopping, are developing rapidly, changing the way people learn, work, shop and play. When leading politicians and leaders of industry speak of the global information society or the information superhighway, they have in mind a much more advanced version of what is currently available via Internet, online databases and CD-ROM. They foresee a time, in the relatively near future, when all cultural products are available in digital form, stored in vast searchable databases and delivered via transparent telecommunication networks to high-resolution PCs and television sets. Many librarians and educationalists share this future expectation of access for everyone, to everything, anytime, from anywhere. Publishers around the world are busy establishing how best they can respond to this development.

Although more and more information is being made available in electronic form, the market for printed products continues to grow. So does the market for television, video, film and games. It is not a question of one medium eradicating the other. But there are significant shifts in growth patterns for different publishing products, caused by changes in market behaviour, which publishers

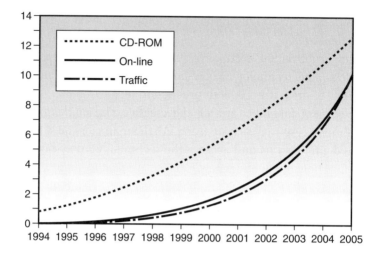

Figure 22 Total revenues from multimedia publishing (US $ billion)
Source: Ovum, 1995

must pay careful attention to as this could have strategic implications and a significant impact upon their sales.

A major challenge for publishers is to acquire the understanding of how to combine different media formats and take advantage of new distribution channels. The publishing process is no longer simple and linear in form. The value and business cycles have become more complex to manage, with many more elements being added. It is necessary to re-define the market and the process of publishing in order to take advantage of the changing market. Publishers need to come up with business strategies that will fit the new market terrain in order to remain competitive.

Many publishers are unwittingly sitting on potential goldmines of poorly exploited copyrights, human talents and resources. But many fail to see how these valuable assets can be optimised in the new networked economy. They simply do not have the vision or management capability to change and expand their business in tune with the changing market. Instead they opt for the ostrich position and try to stick with the old ways. In the short term such a resistant strategy may seem to be holding for some successful publishers. This can be observed in particular in the very successful book publishing industry. But in the long run these publishers will no doubt lose out as the accumulating loss of business opportunities mounts up.

Will the grand old publishing houses still be "grand" in 25 years from now? Will they still produce top-selling titles and have the exclusive rights to mankind's greatest modern literary works? Or will they fail to absorb change, and slowly but surely, see their dominance in the information market diminish? Will they dismiss the great new publishing opportunities as passing fads and gimmicks? If so, more competitive players will be left alone to reap the rewards of what was once a very safe turf where only a limited number of publishers were allowed to play. Already there are many new players on the publishing turf. The clever ones would probably not hesitate to exercise an aggressive acquisition strategy if some of those grand old figures of publishing were to decline the invitation to go digital or delay their involvement. In fact, the take-over or elimination of old players by new competition is now a well-known phenomenon in the publishing industry. The acquisition rate has gone through the roof, particularly during the period 1992–6 and many publishers have gone through several ownership changes.

Traditionally, publishers have been organised in different sectors depending on what they publish and the form of media they publish in, for example, commercial book publishing, academic publishing, STM (scientific, technical and medical) journals and books, magazines, newspapers, photographs or illustrations, classical or popular music, films, programmes for radio or television, videos or games, and so on.

However, the development of digital publishing technologies and the deregulation of markets have removed many of the old boundaries between different publishing activities. The technology and means of production, dissemination and delivery are now often the same for the different types of media products. A digital transmission may contain a television or a radio broadcast, a newspaper, a piece of music, a film, a book, a journal article, a photograph, WWW or Internet pages, or for that matter a telephone conversation. The same transmission network can be used for different types of delivery. The technical skills required for publishing these "strings of digital bits" are very similar too, across the different forms of media.

Understanding process and managing bits

It is no longer so much the nature of the individual types of publishing products or services that matter, as the nature of the market segment for which they are intended. Publishers who may have been very product driven in the past are now recognising the need to be more market driven and customer oriented. Increased competition and fast-changing market dynamics have forced many to review their business strategies and market understanding. Publishing is not limited to publishing individual titles and building up collections or lists of individual titles. The concept of publishing has expanded from traditional "bulk publishing" to

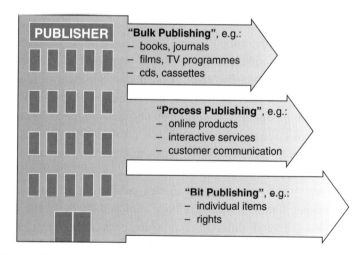

Figure 23   The triple concept of publishing
© A. Leer/Scandinavian University Press, 1996

what may be referred to as "process publishing" and "bit publishing".

Publishers will continue to publish "bulk" products such as books, magazines, television programmes, videos, music and software on compact discs. But they are also increasingly developing various services as part of their product portfolio. The idea of making so-called "hybrid products" is receiving a lot of attention. A "hybrid product" is a series of interlinking publishing products packaged together to add more value and functionality. For instance, it could consist of a textbook in science, a multimedia science encyclopaedia on CD-ROM, a science video game, online tutorials and interactive laboratory on Internet. In interactive online publishing, the process of interaction with the customer can itself be a publishing product.

In addition to "bulk" and "process", publishers are increasingly dealing in "bits" too. Publishers are keen to exploit their intellectual properties. They are often in an excellent position to take advantage of the growing market demand for material which can be used as part of multimedia products or included in various types of compilations of information or entertainment. Publishers can supply endless "bits of stuff"; they can sell and license rights for single parts of publications, for example to be used in other media or by individual customers for some particular purpose.

Publishers are finding opportunities to extend their branding by developing product lines of related and integrated products and services. By July 1996, over 800 newspapers around the world had launched their newspapers online. Many of them were quick to discover that online newspaper publishing opens up entirely new ways of delivering publishing content. It goes far beyond making electronic versions of the printed format.

There seem to be three different trends emerging amongst newspaper publishers: One is simply to offer electronic access to the printed newspaper edition. Publishers either put their newspapers up on the net themselves or they chose to do so via an online service provider or they do both.

The second trend focuses on the concept of personalised newspapers. This idea was pioneered at the Media Lab at the Massachusetts Institute of Technology in the United States. Readers will tell the publisher details of who they are, their areas of interest, and what sort of information they would like to have in their newspapers. The publisher will use this information to build up "personal reader profiles" and deliver individual editions to each individual reader, newspapers tailored to individual preferences and tastes. It is a sort of "Daily Me" type of newspaper, rather than a "Daily World". Although these experiments are exciting, one cannot help wondering what the world would be like if people only heard, read and saw what they had indicated an interest in, what they had asked for. Would it be the end of personal growth?

The third trend is to develop hybrid products and combine the print edition with online news services, archives of back issues/programmes on CD-ROM. It advances searchable databases targeted at professional and academic markets.

Many publishers are building product portfolios based upon flexible lists of titles targeted at specific customer groups. They are developing powerful product lines where individual titles can be quickly added, amended or removed, according to market demand. The ability to optimise and develop brands is essential in order to succeed and attract consumer loyalty in an ever more competitive market-place.

But not all publishers find this transition to the new networked economy easy. Over the years, many traditional publishers have adopted an introvert perspective of the world. They do not venture often enough outside their traditional publishing culture and activity. As a result they fail to take notice of just how much things have changed.

It is a perspective that assumes linearity and passivity in terms of relationships in the value-circle. Authors are there as suppliers of raw material: the image of the author as creative water tap in the publisher's kitchen, publishers being able to turn on the tap of cre-

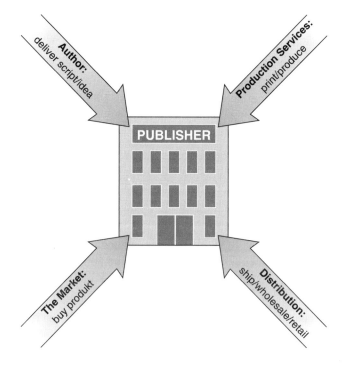

Figure 24 The introvert perspective of the "old style" publisher
© A. Leer/Scandinavian University Press, 1996

ativity whenever they need it. Production services are simply mechanical facilities to get a job done. The distribution system moves the product out the way they have always done. The object of the relationship with the customer is the purchase of the product. It is a one-way story all the way.

However this introvert perspective is no longer sustainable. The development of the information market has changed and broadened the traditional roles of the players in the market-place and their relationships. The process of invention, production, distribution and consumption is no longer simple and linear.

It is often a challenge for larger publishers to see the business opportunity of grouping together individual titles which traditionally belong in different corners of the enterprise. They need to re-

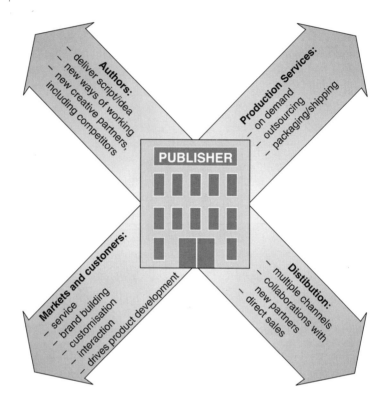

Figure 25 The extrovert perspective of the "new style" publisher
© A. Leer/Scandinavian University Press, 1996

organise internally in order to improve the exploitation of their intellectual property rights. Strategic portfolio management of rights is essential in order to succeed in building dynamic lists across different subject areas and editorial groups.

Mixed media product lines and the expansion of different forms of publishing cannot be achieved without new skills and resources. Consequently publishers enter into all sorts of collaborations with external partners, from so-called third-party multimedia developers, to network operators, service providers, software companies, and so on. Managing external partnerships well is critical and the key to long-term success.

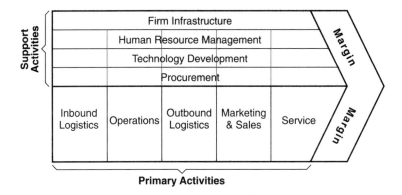

Figure 26 The traditional generic value-chain
Source: Michael E. Porter, *Competitive Advantage*, 1985

But publishers also need to develop good internal partnerships between different business units within their own organisation, in order to pool the necessary expertise and resources to innovate, spot opportunities and achieve critical mass.

Changing business models

Established concepts used for developing business models frequently no longer fit as they do not accommodate the new market dynamics. For instance, widely used concepts such as the "value-chain" and the "product life-cycle" presuppose a notion of linearity and dictate a sequential order in the business process that can go very wrong when transferred into business models. To take the example of publishing, the value-chain for publishing is

Figure 27 A traditional value-chain of publishing
© A. Leer/Scandinavian University Press, 1996

often described in terms of three main parts: creative input, editing/production and distribution/output.

With the advent of electronic publishing and the global information society, the framework for creating value looks more like a circle. So it would be more useful to develop concepts of value-circles or value matrixes. And as for the "product life-cycle", this is a concept borrowed from biology. It implies that something is "born", goes through the process of "growing up", "matures" and inevitably "dies". There are of course well-proven business strategies on offer to deal with each of these four evolutionary stages in the life of the product.

However, the idea that the life of a product should follow the four main phases of biological life-forms is quite absurd, if you think about it. Why do we accept such a notion? Is it useful? There

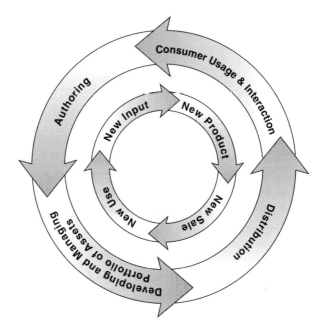

Figure 28 The new value-circle of publishing
© A. Leer/Scandinavian University Press, 1996

THE BUSINESS CHALLENGE 87

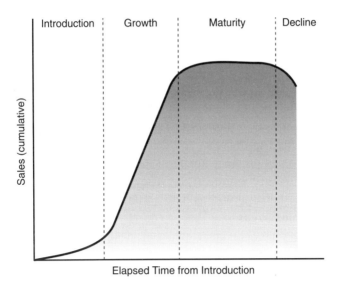

Figure 29 The old concept of the product life-cycle
Source: Michael J. Baker, *Marketing: Theory and Practice*, 1976

are plenty of examples of products that never die or seem to leap into the market without any "growing pains". There are also examples of "dead" products coming to life and finding a place in the market.

The "product life-cycle" concept can be dangerous because it can cause vision impairment. It often narrows down the scope of perceived market opportunity. The "product life-cycle" can stop us from understanding how products "live" in the market. One of the important challenges in the networked economy is to optimise the value of assets by understanding how they interrelate and can be combined. Quite often this will extend and enrich the "life" of individual products, that is, products will not die, but change and evolve into something new.

The impact of digital technologies and networks are changing the way in which value is created, added and exploited in the market. We need to revise and extend existing concepts and business models and develop new ones if necessary. But we must be careful not to throw the baby out with the bath water. There are essential resources, basic functions, fundamental principles and areas of responsibility which still apply and need to remain intact. They are tried and tested by history and looked after by traditional industrial sectors and regulatory bodies.

We shall still see authorship, publishing, advertising, retailing and electronic transmission and delivery (broadcasting/telecommunications) as primary functions of the networked economy. Libraries will also continue to play a key role both as custodians of our cultural heritage and as active information providers in all kinds of subject areas.

Chapter 3
Content management and intellectual property rights

Trading information and media as digital bits

The network grid of the global information society will be used as another set of marketing channels for trading all kinds of assets. Manufacturers of goods and retailers from a wide range of industries are already using the Internet as a new form of catalogue shopping, allowing consumers to window-shop via their PC or television screens and place orders for goods to be paid for and delivered by traditional means. However, increasingly the main economic activity over these global networks will be the trading of information and media assets.

An "information asset" can be defined as any tradeable media commodity of commercial value in any medium or combinations of media formats (text, pictures, sound, moving images). Here we take "information" in its broadest sense and consider the transactional process for trading all kinds of information and media assets in international digital networks. Many basic mechanisms and procedures involved in such information transactions can be applied generically, regardless of what type of information asset is being exchanged.

However, special attention and focus is given to information assets which can be defined as intellectual properties, in particular assets protected by copyright and related rights. This is necessary, because it is in the area of protected information and intellectual property rights that the problems for transactional systems and global information exchange accumulate, posing many challenges in terms of achieving competitiveness and growth in the information market.

The trouble with information assets

Most economists are not very fond of information assets. They are harder to understand and differ from other commodities in many respects. Information assets are different from other commodities because:

- information has an intangible nature;
- information is considered a public good and a political instrument of democracy;
- information cannot be owned;
- information is vulnerable and subject to human communication skills; and
- information is expressed in tangible forms that are exclusively protected.

The degree of tangibility required for value assessment is often hard to define. And information assets usually fit rather poorly with established economic models. For instance, consider this dilemma: If I have some information I know will be of value to you, I will have to tell you about it. But once I have told you about it, you already know, so you may not need to buy my information any more.

Therefore the "information asset owner" will have to depend on marketing resources to persuade the market that what he has is worth purchasing, that is, know the knowledge of exactly how and how much to tell you for free so that you will want to come back and buy some more.

Information is one of the main pillars of democracy and the right of public access to information is a fundamental principle in all democratic nations, and also defined and cemented at the international level in the 1946 United Nations' Universal Declaration of Human Rights.

Another challenge for the information market is that information cannot legally be owned. It follows that what cannot be owned cannot be stolen. The concept of theft cannot be applied to something which cannot be owned.[39] Only certain rights attached to defined types of information can be legally owned, not the information itself.

Information is generated and received by human individuals and will consequently be subject to various sets of communication criteria in order to gain value. This is also the case with intelligent computing, where the terms of communicating information will have been to a large extent pre-defined by human program design. This makes information vulnerable and dependent on individual human skills at both the producer and the consumer end. For instance, information is only as good as its source. The journalist may have misjudged a report, or a film may fail at the box office because it was not interpreted and received in the way intended. It is often hard to establish the real value of information until the transaction has taken place and the information has been consumed.

The final characteristic distinguishing information assets from other commodities is the monopoly rights that may be attached to these assets when the expression of the information appears in tangible forms defined as intellectual properties that have been granted exclusive legal protection.

The economic value of information increases according to the degree of tangibility that can be defined and attached to the information. There are other dynamic factors – such as: brands, the credibility of the information provider, the nature of the content, and market demand – that influence and determine the economic value of information assets.

The intellectual property system is a fundamental economic strategy enabling industries as well as individual authors and information providers to secure the value of their core assets. However, intellectual property rights (IPRs) are not the only means of protecting the value of information assets. Commercial enterprise is continuously looking for new ways of protecting the value of information assets in the struggle to achieve competitive advan-

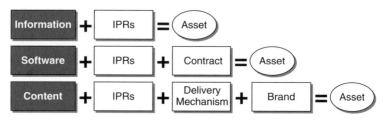

Figure 30 The aggregate nature of information assets
© A. Leer/Scandinavian University Press, 1996

tage, for example by strategic marketing techniques such as brand-building, the creation of "hybrid products" that have a modular product design with interlinking features and add-on functions, bundling and packaging of products and services, lock-in measures, proprietary technology or process solutions, and more.

Global networks such as those available through Internet, including the World Wide Web (WWW), open up many new opportunities for marketing information assets. The way in which information is presented, distributed, sold and used is different in the networked environment as opposed to the traditional market place. For instance, consider the role of publishing. With electronic access to complex databases, almost anybody will be able to put together new editorial products, create information assets and sell them to the market. The process of publishing is changing and electronic publishing requires new kinds of authorship and new ways of publishing.

The intellectual property system

Intellectual property rights (IPRs) represent fundamental trade mechanisms, facilitating a protected commercial exchange of information assets. The trading of intellectual property commodities – information assets – is becoming more and more significant in the world economy. For instance, in the European Union copyright and related rights alone account for 5 per cent of gross domestic product (GDP).[40]

"Intellectual property" has been defined as "works of the mind" in "tangible form",[41] for instance literary and artistic works, photographs, films, video, music on records, tapes or discs, architectural drawings, industrial designs and patterns, computer software and database programs. The history of the "intellectual property system" began with the Industrial Revolution and the need to protect commercial exploitation of intellectual property, for instance new industrial inventions. Patents were the first form of legal protection to be conceptualised in English law. Copyright came much later.

> . . . it is useful to conceive of the system as a set of incentives and rewards designed to affect the behaviour of individuals or organised groups engaged in creative or inventive activities. This system is divided into five interrelated parts:
>
> 1 Policy goals that it seeks to accomplish
> 2 Property rights that provide incentives and rewards
> 3 Operating rules
> 4 Mechanisms by which policy goals are achieved
> 5 A realm of people and activities that the system is designed to influence.[42]

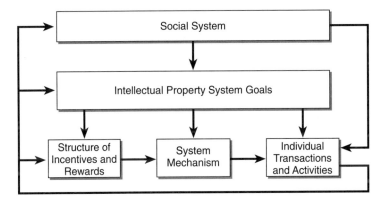

Figure 31 The intellectual property system
Source: Office of Technology Assessment, US Administration

In other words, the intellectual property system exists in order to protect, enforce and develop "intellectual property rights". The system is concerned with three different levels of activity, balancing social, economic and political interests, the levels of policy, principles, and rules. The system consequently consists of a number of laws, policy and trade agreements, as well as relationships between interested parties, tradition and practice, on both a national and an international level. It includes the legal and political structure of patents, copyrights, trade secrecy, contract and competition law.

It is increasingly difficult to maintain the traditional distinctions between the various components of the intellectual property rights system, for example, on a functional level between patent and copyright, and on a policy level between the World Intellectual Property Organisation (WIPO) and the World Trade Organisation (WTO formerly GATT). This shifting of borders is particularly interesting to observe in the area of computer software, databases and electronic publishing where owners of new forms of intellectual property have to "choose" categories and lobby for measures of protection of different types.

Copyright: the critical trading mechanism of the global information market

It is widely recognised and agreed that copyright is the most appropriate set of intellectual property rights for multimedia and information assets in digital form. Much effort has been invested at both national and international levels over the past few years to develop copyright law to accommodate the impact of digital technology.

However, although copyright law is reasonably up to date and harmonised on an international level, the interpretation, administration and practice of the laws vary tremendously depending on cultural traditions, national domain and individual perceptions. This causes enormous problems on the practical level, when industry and commerce attempt to establish services and create activities that require a global administration of intellectual property rights.

If a group of leading representatives of industry, authors and publishers, legal experts, government and educational could come together to discuss the critical issues currently facing them, copyright would feature high on the agenda. If you asked them to share their perspectives and definitions of "copyright", the result would be a lively debate with a wide range of differing opinions. There would almost certainly be as many different definitions of copyright as there were people in the room.

In other words, there exist several different and sometimes competing perspectives of copyright, which are important to appreciate in order to achieve a common understanding. Paul Goldstein, one of the world's leading legal authorities on copyright, has pointed this out.

> What is copyright? A policy maker in the United States will tell you that copyright is an instrument of consumer welfare, stimulating the production of the widest possible array of literary and artistic works at the lowest possible price. But ask the question of a practitioner on the European continent, and he will tell you that copyright is at best a watered down version of author's right – the grand civil law tradition that places the author, not the consumer, at the centre of protection. A low protectionist will tell you that copyright is a monopoly that undesirably drives up the price of goods in the market place. A high protectionist will tell you that copyright is a property right – no more, no less – and one without which we would have very few creative works in the market place.
>
> Ask the question of a United States trade official and she will tell you that copyright is one of the strongest net contributors to the nation's balance of trade. Ask the question of a school teacher in Thailand and he will tell you that copyright is what stand in the way of getting textbooks into the hands of his students. Ask the question of an anthropologist digging through the remains of the 1976 Copyright Act a century from now and she might tell you that copyright is a symbol of a nation's cultural aspirations. Ask the same question today of a manufacturer of novelty knick-knacks and he will tell you that copyright is simply what enables him to meet his payroll at the end of the week.[44]

Who to believe? An in-depth study of the evolution of copyright will reveal they are all right and they are all wrong. What usually happens is that people will tend to define copyright from their own viewpoint and on the basis of self-interest. The consequence is that most people have only a fragmented perception of copyright and fail to see the overall picture, which would reveal the complete function and meaning of the term.

Copyright is not about the right to copy; as the term so misleadingly suggests. Copyright reflects a nation's cultural ambition and the level of consumer welfare and it provides the fundamental conditions for trade. Copyright is thus about many different rights, economic as well as moral:

1 the right to possess or physically control something
2 the right to use or enjoy its benefits
3 the right to manage or decide how it is to be used
4 the right to receive income from it
5 the right to consume or destroy it
6 the right to modify it
7 the right to transfer it
8 the right to distribute it
9 the right to exclude others from using it.[45]

Paul Goldstein offers a more complete definition when he states that "copyright" is about authorship:

> By "authorship" I mean authors communicating as directly as circumstance allows with their intended audiences. Copyright sustains the very heart and essence of authorship by enabling this communication, this connection. It is copyright that makes it possible for audiences – markets – to form for an authors work and it is copyright that makes it possible for publishers to bring these works to market.[46]

This perception of copyright as a precondition for trade is becoming increasingly important. The definition should also be extended to include copyright not only as a condition for trade, but also as an object of trade.

The origin of copyright

England was the first country in the world to develop "copyright legislation": this served as a model for development in other countries. The term "copyright" was coined in 15th-century England after William Caxton introduced the printing press there in 1477, although the term has not been noted until much later in register books in the 1670s. Bookbinders, printers and booksellers were organised in the Stationers' Company which succeeded in lobbying for the very first exclusive copyright and was granted a royal charter in 1557. The charter limited almost all printing to the members of the Stationers' Company and gave them the power to identify and destroy unlawful books to be found anywhere in the kingdom. This historic origin of copyright is often forgotten, it is important to remember because it demonstrates the fact that, from the very start, there has been an intimate relationship between copyright legislation, market conditions and the political environment. The stationers' desire for a market monopoly on print and publishing coincided with the political desire to control the output of the press: ". . . the stationers immediately proved to be a valuable ally of the government in its campaign to suppress dissent by controlling the output of the press (which, indeed, had been Mary [Tudor's] motive in granting the royal charter."[47]

At first, the protection of copyright was given to the stationers, or in modern terms, the publishers.

> The call for effective protection in statutory form, when it came, did not emanate from authors, a body which has historically been disinterested in acting for its own interest. It arrived eventually when commercial men moved in to develop writers' works in saleable form, which came about with the invention of printing. Naturally the State swiftly came to appreciate the political and economic significance of the new invention, and at an early stage the king assumed the monopoly of granting licenses to print.[48]

Copyright in the early days was not an "author's right" or indeed a "user's right", nor was it a political tool to stimulate progress in society, which is the intent of modern copyright law. The first copyright was clearly limited to two functions: the stationers' economic right of market monopoly and the government's right to full censorship of the press.

What has become known as the "stationers' copyright" lasted for nearly two centuries and had a strong influence on successive laws, including the current copyright law, which also reflects the origin of copyright and the legal heritage. Copyright legislation has been developed and revised as a consequence of changes that have taken place both in the market-place and in the political environment. The historic developments in the West during the rise of Protestantism, the Reformation and the Age of Enlightenment had a profound impact on politics, trade, commerce and society as a whole. Consequently the issue of copyright was also affected.

After almost 200 years of the stationers' copyright monopoly, coupled with censorship and central control of the press, protest and frustration had accumulated. One has to remember the political environment during these times which had a strong progressive movement favouring knowledge and learning in a free competitive society – a movement which was contradictory to the copyright policy of the time. The major objection was against the power of the Stationers' Company and the fact that they abused their monopoly status through artificially high prices. This objection finally resulted in the stationers losing the public legal protection in 1694. For some time the stationers petitioned Parliament to reinstate the censorship laws and revive their public legal protection. But when they failed they changed their strategy and started to use the authors as an excuse to bring back copyright. This worked and brought about the copyright law often referred to as the first in "modern" copyright history – the Statute of Anne, passed in England in 1709 which came into force in 1710. Although this was the world's first statutory copyright legislation, it is dangerous to mark this as the beginning, since the preceding two centuries of the stationers' copyright contain important influences and valuable lessons for the intellectual property system of today.

The Statute of Anne marks the second step in the evolution of copyright and introduces the use of copyright as a trade-regulation concept. It also introduces the concept of "author's right" and of copyright as a political device for the public good through stimulating the creation of works and encouraging learning. Indeed the full title of the Statute reads: "An act for the encouragement of learning, by vesting the copies of printed books in the authors or purchasers of such copies, during the times therein mentioned".

In the United States, the Statute of Anne was in effect imported into US copyright law and served in full as the model of the first National Copyright Act in 1790, which was later revised several times. American copyright tradition is coloured by the fact that the initiators had the experience of the authoritarian politics, tyranny of censorship and religious fanaticism of 14th–17th century England fresh in their minds. In fact, copyright law is directly connected to the First Amendment of the US Constitution: Section 8 of Article I of the constitution, authorises Congress to grant exclusive ownership rights of writings and inventions for a limited period of time. The purpose was twofold: 1) to foster the progress of science and the useful arts, and 2) to encourage the creation and dissemination of information and knowledge to the public.

Copyright in the international environment

Europe has had a different copyright tradition and direction from that of the United States, although this is less obvious today. Continental European copyright law, in particular in France, has focused very strongly on the moral rights of the author – droit d'auteur. Anglo-American copyright law has until recently not included moral rights to the same degree, but rather focused on the economic rights.

Since intellectual property is traded and used extensively across national borders, it has been necessary to establish both bilateral and multilateral agreements on an international level. The first and single most important international convention is the Berne Convention. The international issues of copyright used to be almost exclusively controlled by the United Nations through the Berne Convention administered by WIPO (World Intellectual Property Organisation) and the Universal Copyright Convention administered by UNESCO (United Nations' Educational, Scientific and Cultural Organisation), both set up under the UN.

However, today the international picture is much more complex and includes many other important actors. As intellectual property has grown to become a large proportion of nations' gross national products, almost every major intergovernmental agency is now dealing with issues concerning copyright. This includes for instance the EU, WTO, OECD, UNCTAD, COE, EFTA and several others.

The Berne Convention

The Berne Union was established in 1886. The initiative came originally from the International Literary and Artistic Association which had proposed a draft and eventually succeeded in getting the Swiss government to call an international meeting. As of 1996, a total of 84 countries have joined the Berne Union, and adhered to the Berne Convention and its various protocols. The Berne Convention offers the highest level of international copyright protection and it also serves as a model for national legislation in many countries. The Convention has been revised many times and there are several additional protocols to the original 1886 text, most recently the protocol concerning computer software.

The Universal Copyright Convention

The Universal Copyright Convention (UCC) was set up in 1952, primarily to offer registration and administration of copyright and

CONTENT MANAGEMENT 101

Country	Berne	UCC	Paris	Country	Berne	UCC	Paris
Algeria		X	X	Lebanon	X	X	
Andorra		X		Liberia		X	X
Argentina	X	X	X	Libya	X		
Australia	X	X	X	Liechtenstein	X	X	X
Austria	X	X	X	Luxembourg	X	X	X
Bahamas	X	X	X	Madagascar	X		X
Bangladesh		X		Malawi		X	X
Barbados	X	X		Mali	X		X
Belgium	X	X	X	Malta	X	X	X
Belize		X		Mauritania	X		X
Benin	X		X	Mauritius		X	X
Brazil	X	X	X	Mexico	X	X	X
Bulgaria	X	X	X	Monaco	X	X	X
Burkina Faso	X			Morocco	X	X	X
Burundi		X		Netherlands	X	X	X
Cameroon	X	X	X	New Zealand	X	X	X
Canada	X	X	X	Nicaragua		X	
Central African Republic	X		X	Niger	X		X
Chad	X		X	Nigeria		X	X
Chile	X	X		Norway	X	X	X
Colombia		X		Panama		X	
Congo	X		X	Pakistan	X	X	
Costa Rica	X	X		Paraguay		X	
Cuba		X	X	Peru		X	
Cyprus	X		X	Philippines	X	X	X
Czechoslovakia	X	X	X	Poland	X	X	X
Democratic Kampuchea		X		Portugal	X	X	X
Denmark	X	X	X	Romania	X		X
Dominican Republic		X	X	Rwanda	X		X
Ecuador		X		San Marino			X
Egypt	X		X	Senegal	X	X	X
El Salvador		X		Singapore			
Fiji	X	X		South Africa	X		X
Finland	X	X	X	Soviet Union		X	X
France	X	X	X	Spain	X	X	X
Gabon	X		X	Sri Lanka	X	X	X
Germany	X	X	X	Suriname	X		X
Ghana		X	X	Sweden	X	X	X
Greece	X	X	X	Switzerland	X	X	X
Guatemala		X		Syria			X
Guinea	X	X	X	Tanzania			X
Haiti		X	X	Thailand	X		
Holy See	X	X	X	Togo	X		X
Hungary	X	X	X	Trinidad and Tobago			X
Iceland		X		Tunisia	X	X	X
India	X	X		Turkey	X		X
Indonesia			X	Uganda			X
Iran			X	United Kingdom	X	X	X
Iraq			X	United States		X	X
Ireland	X	X	X	Upper Volta			X
Israel	X	X	X	Uruguay	X		X
Italy	X	X	X	Venezuela	X	X	
Ivory Coast	X		X	Viet Nam			X
Japan	X	X	X	Yugoslavia	X	X	X
Jordan			X	Zaire	X		X
Kenya		X	X	Zambia		X	X
Korea, Republic of			X	Zimbabwe	X		X
Laos		X					

Figure 32 Overview of member countries of the Berne Convention and the Universal Copyright Convention (UCC)

Source: Office of Technology Assessment, US Administration

to offer a lower level of protection than the Berne Convention in order to attract a wider range of member states. It included, for instance the United States, the Soviet Union, China and some developing countries, which were not members of the Berne Convention at the time. However, today most nations are members of the Berne Union, including the United States, which joined in 1989.

Consideration	Copyright	Patent	Trade Secrecy	Contract Law
Duration	50, 75 or 100 yrs	17 years	Until disclosed	As agreed
Enforceable	Worldwide*	Nationwide	State-by-state	Worldwide*
Acquired by	Act of creation	Application	Agreement	Agreement
Lost by	Improper notice	Legal challenge	Disclosure	Expiry or breach
Cost to obtain	Trivial	Significant	Trivial	Low
Cost to maintain	Trivial	Trivial	Significant	Low
Cost to defend	Moderate	Moderate	Significant	Moderate
Protects/prevents:				
Ideas & designs	No	Yes	Yes	Yes
Copying	Yes	Yes	No	Yes
Use	No	Yes	No	Yes
Independent invention	No	Yes	No	No
Distribution	Yes	Yes	Yes	Yes
Material must be:				
Unique	No	Yes	No	No
Novel	No	Yes	No	No
Used in business	No	No	Yes	No
Not generally known	No	Yes	Yes	No
Remedies available:				
Injunction	Yes	Yes	Yes	Yes
Statutory damages	Yes	No	No	No
Attorney's fees	Yes	Yes	No	No
Suitable for:				
Retail sales	Yes	Yes	No	No
Licensed use	Yes	Yes	Yes	Yes
Subject matter covered	Works of authorship *with exceptions	1. Machines 2. Articles of manufacture 3. Processes 4. Compositions of matter	Valuable business information	Anything *with exceptions

Figure 33 Overview of legal protections
Source: Ernest E. Keet, *Preventing Piracy*, 1985

Legislation in the mould

There are currently several pieces of draft legislation on the table at both national and international level in order to respond to the impact of new technology on intellectual property rights and the protection of information assets. The EU Database Directive of 1995 is expected to have a significant impact on the information market, since it introduces a sui generis right (that is, not an intellectual property right) whereby the "manufacturer" of a database will be able to prevent unauthorised acts of "extraction or reutilization" of that collection for a period of 15 years. According to article 6 in this proposal, in respect of databases the following acts will be protected:

1 The temporary and permanent reproduction of the database by any means and in any form, in whole or in part;
2 the translation, adaptation, arrangement and any other alteration of the database;
3 the reproduction of the results of any of the acts listed in (1) or (2);
4 any form of distribution to the public, including the rental, of the database or copies thereof; and
5 any communication, display or performance of the database to the public.

The intention of the directive is to provide legal protection of databases that may not be covered under copyright laws, and thereby to encourage investment and growth in the European information market. However, opponents claim that the directive will create legal uncertainty concerning what types of databases are protected under which laws. In many EU member-states, databases are defined as compilations of works that are covered by both national copyright laws and the Berne Convention. Opponents in the US market see the directive as an attempt to protect and favour European industry, and question whether it is in breach with the GATT agreement on Trade Related spects of Intellectual Property Rights (TRIPS).

The publishing industry is well aware of its need of and dependency on statutory protection. It is also lobbying for the inclusion of a "new" right: the publisher's right, justified on the basis of the increasing amount of creative effort that the publisher contributes in the process of publishing. In fact much material is authored and created by the publisher's own staff. The layout and the typeface of a book has long been the debate of copyright claims. But there is much more to the publisher's role of creating works in electronic multimedia publishing.

Two other important documents released in 1995 will also have a significant impact on the development of policy and regulatory frameworks for the GII. They are:

- the *White Paper on Intellectual Property and the Global Information Infrastructure*, published by US Department of Commerce in July 1995; and
- the *Green Paper on Intellectual Property and the Global Information Society*, published by the European Commission in August 1995.

Copyright as a trade mechanism

As a trade mechanism, copyright can be used as a tool in a number of constructive ways, but it can also be applied in a negative fashion. On the one hand copyright provides incentives and rewards to copyright-holders, stimulating the production of works. It also relates to the price mechanism and provides contractual relationships in the value-circle of the publishing business. It organises the transfer of values in a manner that is agreeable to the parties concerned.

On the other hand, copyright can be applied in a destructive manner, for instance as a barrier to trade, by monopolising information value, by restricting public and corporate access to information, by denying the poor and less skilled (individual, company or nation) from acquiring knowledge, by encouraging the gap between the knowledge-rich and the knowledge-poor.

Copyright can also demoralise individuals' attitudes towards usage of information, by interpreting (and even creating) laws and practices in the copyright enforcement system which undermine the constructive intent of copyright. Typical examples are overprotective operational procedures in copyright control that are experienced as unreasonable and insulting by users, as commonly seen in the wording of the shrink-wrapped license agreements that follow some software packages and by some collecting societies in the area of reprography (photocopying).

> Copyright and free-speech rights (a phrase we use to encompass booth the free speech and free press clauses of the First Amendment) can be viewed as opposite sides of the same coin. The former is a matter of proprietary rights, the latter of society's political rights. They are bonded because both deal with the flow of information, one in the interest of profit, the other in the interest of freedom. The profit motive, however, is not a wholly reliably monitor. Like the locks in a canal, it may facilitate the flow of information, or in fact in may serve to dam that flow. This explains why the regulatory aspects of copyright must govern the proprietary aspects, for the early history of copyright – which we ignore at our peril – demonstrates how closely copyright and free speech values were (and are) connected.[49]

Copyright as an object of trade

Copyright is also increasingly becoming an end in itself for several commercial enterprises. Copyright can be segmented into a number of different rights products eligible for trade in the market. Another growing area of importance is the process of administrating and clearing copyright. Due to the advances in electronic media, there are a growing number of activities in this field, which opens up a challenging market opportunity for the publishing industry.

The current system of copyright administration and clearance

Copyright administration and clearance is a far from homogeneous market. There are different models and practices established in different parts of the world. In general, the variety of organisations involved – agencies, interest groups and business operations – are many times more complex in Europe than in the United States. The distinction between political, social and economic motives of some of these organisations may be difficult as they often operate in a grey area, between acting as self-interest groups and exploiting commercial market opportunities.

The concept of collecting societies was first established in the area of music in the mid-19th century, primarily in response to the development of broadcasting and recording technologies. Other areas such as literary and dramatic works followed suit. Publishers, authors and composers formed separate organisations whose prime task was to administer, clear copyright and ensure that the respective copyright-holders received economic compensation for the use of their works.

Today there is a number of such collecting societies primarily concerned with collecting and distributing copyright fees. As the number of rights has expanded, so has the number of copyright organisations. Attached to the various rights one will often find a corresponding copyright organisation. For instance the 'performing rights' in music are represented on an international level by the International Confederation of Societies of Authors and Composers (CISAC). Its membership consists of national organisations from all over the world. Other copyright organisations, for instance in the field of drama, film and television rights, are organised in a similar manner.

The evolution of copyright organisation is a fascinating study of how technology has been allowed to directly influence the organisational structure. Every time a new medium has emerged, the response has been to establish a new collecting society, rather than to build on existing structures. This is no doubt weakening the effectiveness of the copyright business and will cause more and more problems as the previously distinguishable technologies merge into one multimedia industry.

The development of the photocopier machine is a very good example. When Xerox launched the first photocopier, and thereby revolutionised information processing, copyright-holders responded true to tradition by setting up a new type of collecting society called a reproduction rights organisation (RRO). Throughout the world national RROs were set up to license the photocopying of protected information and to combat the escalating growth of unauthorised copying and piracy. Although many of the RROs are organised in a common international forum called IFRRO (International Federation of Reproduction Rights Organisations), this does not necessarily mean that they share common operational procedures. In fact there are at least four very different models which can be categorised as follows.

The Anglo-American model of reproduction rights organisation

This model is based on a system of voluntary contracts and the RROs enter into agreement with both individual rights-holders and organisations representing rights-holders (collective agreements). Collection and distribution of remuneration (fees and royalties) are based on statistical surveys. Statistical data will provide title-specific information allowing for the estimation of the level of intensity of use, which again determines the remuneration to individual rights-holders.

The German-Spanish model

In Germany and Spain there is statutory provision for the collection of a levy on the sales of photocopying machines. The size of the levy is determined by regulation and varies according to the type, capacity and performance capability of the equipment. It will also vary according to location and use. The levy is justified on the basis that private and personal copying is hard to track. Licensing fees for volume copying and systematic use of photocopiers are also determined by regulation. Distribution of remuneration is based on statistical surveys and is apportioned to rights-holders according to agreed source codes and types of protected material used.

The Dutch model

In the Netherlands the RRO operates under a statutory licensing system principally in the government and educational area. The law authorises the users to copy as long as remuneration is made to respective rights-holders. This affects the rights of foreign rights-holders as well. The size of remuneration is set by regulation apart from the copying of course material and readers/basic textbooks, which are negotiated.

The Nordic model

The Nordic model, or more precisely the model of Norway, Sweden and Finland, is significantly different. These RROs will only enter into agreements with organisations representing a substantial proportion of rights-holders, for instance the national association of journalists, editors, authors or publishers. Individual rights-holders cannot enter into an agreement directly, only through the respective trade organisation. In Norway the RRO is registered as a monopoly.

This model is the basis for the 'extended collective license system', which means that whether the rights-holder is organised or not, they still fall under the responsibility of the RRO that is negotiating on his or her behalf. However, the remuneration collected is distributed to the RRO member organisations and the distribution data is not title-specific. This means that there is no individual tracking or identification of protected works. The individual rights-holders can only get access to the remuneration through a process of application for various grants announced by the rights-holders' organisations.

The publishers receive allocations of remuneration based on industry statistics. The distribution of remuneration to the member organisation is based on statistical surveys identifying the volume of types of material copied, for example, press articles, fiction, sheet music or academic literature.

This model presupposes a highly organised society where most rights-holders are represented in trade unions and associations. It also assumes that rights-holders are willing to accept collective distribution of fees and give up their individual right to receive compensation for the copying of their works.

The role of collecting societies in an electronic environment

One rather traumatic issue for the RROs is the development of reproduction technology. For instance, the photocopier is now increasingly becoming digital. And a digital copier is also a printer and a computer peripheral. Suddenly the copier is part of the computer network and is a multifunctional piece of technology. It can be a copier, a printer, a fax, a telephone, a computer, a television, and so on, at the touch of a button. Two questions arise: Should collecting societies also license electronic rights? And if so, which collection society should administer which rights?

The technologies and markets may have converged, but the collecting societies certainly have not. What will be the role of RROs when there no longer are photocopiers around? How can the copyright knowledge and resources of the RROs be put to use in the electronic age? Will they start competing with their own members and disintegrate due to internal conflict or will they provide an important service function and aid the members in creating new business areas? In that case how can the competing objectives of the members be resolved and their interests balanced?

The issues at stake are both political and social, but above all they are economic. Automated and collective administration of rights could potentially release substantial potent economic activity and boost growth in the European information market. But many crucial strategic questions remain unresolved concerning how this can be achieved and what the interface between rights-holders and collecting societies should look like in the future.

Chapter 4
Electronic commerce and information transactions

What makes the market work

Before proceeding to examine information transaction and the key issues involved, let us step back for a moment and consider what actually constitutes a market and what makes it all work. What are the basic building-blocks of this market-place and what are the conditions for market efficiency likely to be?

There must be creators, producers, products, intermediaries and consumers. There must also be marketing systems in place to facilitate the exchange of information assets. We need distribution and delivery systems providing access to information and access to consumers. There must be transactional systems to allow for charging and paying. And last, but not least, there must be rules and regulations protecting the integrity of trade from point of creation to point of consumption.

Perhaps one of the most difficult issues concerning the marketing of information assets in electronic form, is the need for quality control, security and authenticity. The consumer needs to know that what he/she orders is what he/she gets. The producer needs to know that what he/she sells arrives intact at the point of delivery. The libraries and museums that are custodians of our cultural heritage need authentic originals in their archives. The students must be taught according to an approved curriculum of verified knowledge. Science, industry and commerce need reliable data and information that has not been tampered with.

As we move from a world of media divergence and clearly distinguishable media outputs (newspapers, books, journals, films) to a networked society of media convergence, of multimedia and telematics applications, the ability to preserve the integrity and continued growth of intellectual creations will be a major challenge.

Traditional media industries – publishers and broadcasters – are experiencing a fragmentation of their products and expressing strong concerns about digital technologies eroding the integrity of works and dissolving traditional media responsibility. Their defence strategy is the continued protection of intellectual property rights, along with the recognition of the role of publishers and broadcasters in a digital environment.

Information transactions defined

An information transaction is defined as a process of value exchange between two parties, whereas value is defined as information assets (including any type of media) and money. The transactional process includes in its simplest form two value transfers – the financial transaction to secure payment for goods and services ordered, and the transfer of the information asset. If the buyer is an end-user this will typically be the case. However, if intellectual property rights are attached to the asset, then there will be a third

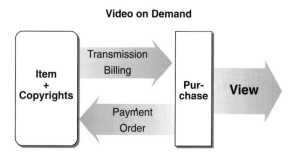

Figure 34 Information transactions: video on demand – pay per view

© A. Leer/Scandinavian University Press, 1996

ELECTRONIC COMMERCE 113

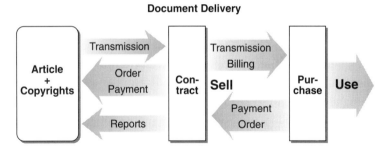

Figure 35 Information transactions: electronic journals – document delivery

© A. Leer/Scandinavian University Press, 1996

value transfer involved to allow for the transfer of rights. The buyer may only want to by the rights and not the actual information. In that case there will be three value transfers: money, rights and a contract. The buyer, perhaps being an agent or a rights broker, may then proceed to sell those rights to another buyer. Or if the buyer is a multimedia programme developer, he or she may want to buy both the information object, the rights and a contract to allow him or her to reuse and sell the material.

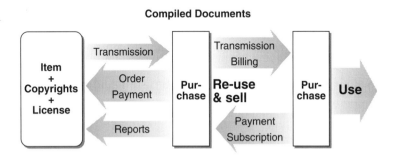

Figure 36 Information transactions: compiled documents – item licensing

© A. Leer/Scandinavian University Press, 1996

The security challenge

There is a lot of debate about the need to make global networks secure. The trading of information assets over global networks raises a number of security problems that need to be resolved in order to facilitate an efficient market. What kind of security we are talking about will to some extent depend on who is talking. "Security" is a very widely used term which carries different meaning for different people. The participants in the global information society security debate come from a variety of different backgrounds and industries, consequently they tend to have different understandings of the security issues involved.

The network provider is concerned with system performance and protection against failure and breakdowns. The bank is concerned with protection of financial transactions. The network service provider is concerned with protection of access and against unauthorised use. The content provider is concerned with protection of intellectual property rights. The law enforcement agency is concerned with access to communication channels and transactional activities to protect law and order. The consumer is concerned with protecting personal information and privacy. Resolving the security problems of the GIS requires a common understanding across the board and an agreement on priorities. In this context it is important that the players involved can appreciate all the issues at stake and not narrow down the implications to what he or she perceives as important from a his or her particular standpoint.

Security concerns are present on several different levels and in relation to a wide range of key functions:

- law enforcement;
- national security;
- payment systems;
- intellectual property rights;
- network access and use of services;

- system performance and quality control;
- data protection; and
- privacy and other consumer rights.

Security features are a fundamental part of transactional systems for information assets. Security specifications for trading information assets in the global information market need to be constructed on the basis of a number of existing standards for network communication, Electronic Data Interchange (EDI), data storage and financial transactions, as well as new standards for more comprehensive data protection, tracking and recording of information usage. The use of cryptography and encryption technology is likely to play a major role in the process of developing the level of security required information transactions.

Cryptography and the use of encryption technology

Cryptography – the science of making (encrypting) and breaking (decrypting) secret codes – has its roots in military defence applications and intelligence surveillance. It has historically been the domain of government agencies concerned with national security, military defence and law enforcement. Today governments are still the largest users of encryption technology, but its use has spread to many other application areas throughout society. The financial service sector is the second largest user. In many countries banks are required by law to provide protection for their customers by implementing specific encryption and security standards to secure transactions and financial information. Cable and satellite television is another sector that uses specific technology, to encrypt television programmes. Many closed communication and computer networks in industry also use some level of encryption to protect their data.

Software for business applications, PCs and other office communication devices is increasingly being shipped with encryption technology embedded either in specially designed security chips or in programs. This causes tension with government agencies whose responsibility it is to control the export and use of encryption technology. In many countries the manufacturing, export and use of high-grade encryption technology are strictly regulated. Some government agencies will license certain industrial sectors to use specific encryption technology. For example, the banking industry is licensed to use encryption technology based on the so-called Data Encryption Standard (DES) (see below).

One big problem for governments is that the regulations governing the use of encryption technology are not up to date in terms of defining the many new encryption techniques and emerging standards. Once again the technology seems to be racing ahead of the legislation. This is a major concern for law enforcement agencies which do not like to lose control over the spread of encryption technology. If encryption technology was freely available in the market, it would also be freely available for criminals involved in organised crime, drug traffic, money laundering, fraud and terrorism.

The regulation and application of encryption technology is a very contentious and difficult issue that needs urgent attention. On the one hand, national security, law and order are at stake, and on the other the ability to create a secure trading environment for the GIS is at stake. Without the use of encryption technology it seems unlikely that information transactions on the GII will be secure. The global information market will not take off without mechanisms being in place to secure such transactions. There are already several examples of companies having to withdraw encrypted products from the market, modify products to render them less secure, or disable encrypted features which would have provided the security that the market requires.[50]

Emerging standards for encrypting information

The market for digital encryption technology is growing at a significant rate, in spite of the uncertain legal environment. In

ELECTRONIC COMMERCE 117

February 1995 there were 219 registered manufacturers and distributors of encryption technology in the European Union alone – including 88 in the United Kingdom, 33 in Germany, and 29 in France. In the United States there were 161 companies while Japan had only 4.[51] The Software Publishers Association has estimated that the potential US share of markets outside the United States for software with encryption capabilities could total US$5 billion by 1997. US software companies currently hold a 70 per cent market share in Europe.

Software encryption is based on two basic types of encryption algorithms: symmetrical-key or single-key encryption and asymmetrical or public-key encryption. In symmetrical encryption the same key is used to encrypt and decrypt the data. The sender and receiver of data must have the same key. Asymmetrical encryption divides the process in two steps, using two associated keys, one private and one public. The private key is known and used only by the owner. The public key can be used by anyone who wants to send encrypted data to the corresponding private key-holder. Only the corresponding private key will be able to decrypt the data. Public-key encryption lets the user encrypt information and messages as well as "signing" them with a "digital signature", by generating a line of text or numbers encrypted with that person's private key. The digital signature can only be decrypted by the sender's public key and it verifies where the information or message came from.

Recently, there has been a lot of activity in this area and there are an increasing number of proposed solutions and actual products available. Most of these software packages offering encryption capability are based on proprietary encryption methods.

Although there is no worldwide agreement on one encryption standard, most products and network applications seem to be based on one of the following "standards" for encryption algorithms:

1 DES (Data Encryption Standard)
  A de jure standard.
  Adopted by the US National Institute of Standards and Technology (NIST); approved for non-classified government data. A symmetrical system developed in 1977 from IBM's Lucifer algorithm. It is the most widely used standard in hardware implementations.
2 RSA
  A de facto standard.
  A comprehensive set of public-key based cryptographic algorithms developed since 1977 at the Massechusetts Institute of Technology, named after the inventors (Rivest-Shamir-Adleman). Several RSA algorithms are protected by US patents held by the PKP (Public Key Partners) company formed jointly by MIT and Stanford University.
3 IDEA (International Data Encryption Algorithm)
  A de facto standard.
  A symmetrical system developed by Lai and Massey in 1991, simple to use and relatively easy to break. Popular in the public domain and amateur applications.

Software with encryption functions will typically integrate the use of encryption algorithms with the vendors' proprietary security features, in a seamless fashion. For instance, a UK-based smart card company called Mondex uses the DES standard with their own added security software. Another company offering secure transactions, Netscape, uses RSA technology in combination with their own proprietary encryption technology called Secure Socket Layer (SSL).

Another software programme that enables users to encrypt information is PGP (Pretty Good Privacy). Developed in 1991 by P. Zimmermann, it combines RSA and IDEA algorithms and has been widely distributed as freeware in the public domain over Internet. Zimmermann had to face legal action over the illegal export of this programme and has been subject to investigation by the US Customs Service. Despite being illegal, PGP is widely used, primarily by individuals wanting to secure their email correspondence, but also by reputable organisations like Amnesty International, and unfortunately also by political extremist groups.

There is a weighty ongoing debate concerning the need for security standards on Internet including the WWW. There seems to be a tug of war between those who advocate an open standard approach and those who advocate a standard approach based on proprietary technology. The well-established online information service providers CompuServe, Prodigy and American Online have invested in Terisa, a company recently set up by EIT and RSA Data Security. to provide technology for secure Internet transactions. The standard recently chosen by the WWW consortium called the S-HTTP (Secure HyperText Transfer protocol) is based on the technology of EIT and RSA.

The standards debate is likely to get even more lively and confused as new proposals are put forward. RSA has been able to dominate the public-key encryption market as it is currently holding US patents on a wide range of applications. However these patents expire during 1997–2001, thus opening up the market for other players.

Information encoding and identifiers

The degree of protection required will vary with the type of asset being traded. Intellectual property assets may require more complex treatment than information assets not protected by IPR. Communities of publishers, authors, broadcasters, composers and libraries, which are all concerned with protecting the integrity of works and the IPRs, have begun to investigate ways of encoding information assets in electronic form and implementing identification mechanisms to enable them to control the use of their works in an electronic environment.

Several standards organisations currently administrating standards for traditional media or communication networks are also busy developing extensions to their existing standards and exploring new ways of marking and tracking digital information. The latter include the well-established standards developed in the 1970s for identifying printed works – the ISBN (International Standard Book Number) code for books and the ISSN (International Standard Serial Number) code for journals, the ISRC (International Standard Recording Code) for identification of recorded music and the SID (Source Identification) code for identification of CD producers, both administered by IFPI (International Federation of the Phonographic Industry). Collecting societies for various media are also busy experimenting with encoding and identification systems.

This field of digital information encoding and identification mechanisms is at a very early stage. The emerging models range from very simple protection of limited information (a header type) to very complex models that aim to control and protect the use of information as far as possible. Technology offers many different techniques for identifying information assets in different electronic media, ranging from so-called watermarking – software that allows identifiers or messages to be embedded in electronic documents, to digital signatures using public-key encryption, to fingerprinting bit-mapped images (FBI), used for identifying images in electronic form.

Mechanisms for encoding and identifying information assets will be of vital importance to the development of the global information market for the purpose of protecting IPR and preserving original assets, as well as securing the integrity and reliability of trade. However, it is important to realise that technology is now making it possible to mark, monitor and control the use of information on a scale never known before. The implications for privacy, data protection and consumer rights need to be considered very carefully.

Transactional systems for network commerce

Much has been written about the commercialisation of Internet and the need for systems that can secure financial transactions and payment for goods and services purchased on the Net. Almost every week, somewhere in Europe, another major conference is organised on the topic of electronic commerce and information transaction. There is a lot of commercial interest in developing and adopting electronic payment systems and there are numerous experiments and trials currently going in Europe, North America, Australia, Japan and Singapore. Initiatives have come from several different camps and the most active companies come from the software industry, telecommunications industry, banking and financial sector, media conglomerates and network operators.

In the popular press there has been a lot of controversial coverage of "virtual money", "cybercash" or "digital money". The topic is "tabloid hot" and it is currently difficult to pick up any computer magazine, business journal or indeed national newspaper without headlines flashing at you, telling tales about virtual shopping and "cyber-commerce". But these entertaining visions of future commerce could be flawed and most of them do not translate very well into the real market-place (or should we say market space).

All this commotion, excitement and sudden interest in transactional systems is symptomatic of the fact that there is an unfulfilled need for new ways of trading information. It is ironic that the actors in the arena that have most drawn attention to this are new entrepreneurial market entrants, "information revolutionaries" and scientists from the academic sector, rather than the traditional players which one would have expected to see take the lead, since they have the most at stake. For instance, the banks were the last to jump on this band-wagon and most of them did so at the invitation of either a software or a telecommunication company.

Existing and emerging transactional mechanisms and models

Over the past two years various models have been developed for handling information transactions in a networked environment. Mechanisms currently available in the market-place can be divided into seven categories. These categories are not mutually exclusive and vendors may come up with business models that require a combination of transactional mechanisms:

- subscription;
- licensing;
- conventional credit/debit cards;
- smart cards;
- third party clearing (brokering);
- electronic cash; and
- electronic cheques.

Subscription and licensing

Subscription and licensing are familiar and well-established transactional methods for trading information online. The customer subscribes to a particular service and/or licensed access and use of specific content. Searching and ordering information may happen online, but the charging, billing and payment usually happen offline using conventional banking and postal services.

Credit and debit cards

The main advantages of credit and debit cards are that they represent:
- familiar transactional concepts;
- a well-proven technology;
- a long established industry;

- well-regulated and managed services; and
- a global, secure and solid infrastructure.

The first credit cards appeared on the US market in the 1920s, initially issued by petrol stations and department stores to enable their customers to use their facilities and purchase products and services using the card rather than cash. These cards could only be used by the customer in the issuer's establishment and the card was limited to a contract between two parties – one merchant and one customer. The first multiparty cards, whereby groups of companies joined to issue a card, were limited to specific markets and could be used for the purpose of travel and entertainment. This was the start of American Express, Diners Club and Carte Blanche – as indeed the names reflect. The first general multipurpose card, BankAmericard, appeared in 1958; Visa and Mastercard followed later.

The credit/debit card business has experienced continuous growth since its inception and gone through many developments, expanding its scope and functionality, adding on more and more features. There is a wide range of cards available, allowing the market to choose between dedicated one-service cards to multiservice cards. There is a growing trend of vendors teaming up with credit card companies to develop and market their own branded cards.

Today all the major credit card companies are working to develop payment systems for electronic commerce for a wired world. They have formed strategic alliances with companies from the telecommunication, software and information industries. New collaborative projects are announced frequently. Current examples are: Visa working with Microsoft and BT, Mastercard with Netscape, American Express with AmericaOnline.

Financial transactions on the Net must be verified and cleared by whoever undertakes to process payments. The existing closed global and secure networks that these credit card companies have built up will be very useful for that purpose, putting them in a strong position as key players in the new market for electronic commerce in open global networks. The cost of building up such large-scale networks for processing transactions would be enormous for any newcomer.

The market environment for financial transactional services is also very competitive and prices have been continually pushed down over the past decade. For instance, redemption of credit card slips was originally around 7 per cent discount, but today credit card discounts average around 2.5 per cent and are expected to drop even further. "Any new payment venture planning a credit card billing model that requires more than 2 per cent discounts for profitability won't be able to compete in the long term."[52]

There are four main disadvantages and problems with the credit model applied to information transactions within global networks:

- lack of security;
- high transaction cost;
- time consuming clearing process; and
- qualifications required to become credit card merchants.

Lack of security. Internet is an open environment with very little security available. Sending credit card details and sensitive financial information over Internet is not safe. Eavesdroppers using cheap TCP/IP traffic monitors and hackers can easily intercept and obtain credit card numbers if they are sent over the Net. This was recently demonstrated with the capture of the American hacker Kevin Mitnick who had a list of over 20,000 customer names and credit card numbers when he was caught.

High transaction costs. The other problem facing the credit card companies is the high cost per transaction, which makes the credit card unsuitable for small transactions. Much of the information asset trade over the global networks is likely to be high volumes of very small transactions between many individual parties. The cost per transaction will outweigh its value. Even if the credit card transaction loop is stretched between clearance and settlement, in order to allow small transactions to aggregate before payments are made, it will not work: aggregated payments still have to be made between one buyer and one merchant.

This has for many years been a familiar problem in the document delivery business – publishers and authors are forever having proceeds outstanding from permissions sold through collecting societies and third-party information services. The long wait for the small cheques has led some publishers to reconsider whether it makes any sense to grant permissions to reproduce their works and make material available though these services. Information services would be much more economically attractive if there was a way of reducing the transaction costs and thereby increasing the profit potential.

Time consuming. Credit/debit cards require authorisation through dial-up communication with clearing services which are networked to banks and credit card companies. The clearing process takes time. The settlement is another time-consuming factor in the payment process as invoices are issued.

Qualifications of credit card merchants. Individuals and small enterprises who may want to trade their information assets on the networks may find it too expensive to offer payment by credit cards and they may not meet the criteria for qualifying as credit card merchants.

Smart cards

Credit/debit card technology has evolved with the development of microchips and computing technology. Smart cards ("chip cards" or "electronic purses") are fitted with a microprocessor that can store value and information as well as provide specified functions. Unlike the credit card, which simply has a magnetic strip with recorded information like a tiny computer disk, the smart card is like a little computer capable of processing information as well as storing it.

There are many different applications and varieties of smart cards available in the market today. There are also a number of trials currently going on to test smart cards in electronic commerce, including services available over Internet.

The smart card provides stored value on a card – or put it another way – it is cash on a card. The card can be "loaded up" with cash by inserting it into smart cash-point machines (ATMs) or by using dedicated terminals and customised telephones. A display will show the balance on the card and debits/credits made. The card can be used for payments for all kinds of goods and services by inserting it in smart card readers which directly debits the card for the requested amount.

The six main advantages of the smart card model are that it:

- builds on the existing credit card industry and infrastructure;
- offers security;
- has lower cost;
- is efficient;
- has ability to handle small transactions; and
- provides added functionality and flexibility.

If the card is stolen, then it is only the current value stored on the card that is lost, as opposed to an entire credit line, which could be the case with credit card fraud.

As there is no need to obtain authorisation, the transaction costs are much lower than with payment systems that require clearance from payment processors.

The clearance and settlement process is instant, making this a highly efficient payment mechanism.

The card can work and be economically viable for small transactions because the transaction costs are low, although profitability with small transactions has not yet been commercially demonstrated with information in electronic form sold over networks – this is currently being explored by a number of banks and software companies.

The ability to design and add different functions to the smart card is perhaps the most important feature of all. Because the card is like a miniature computer, information and special instructions can be received, stored, processed and transmitted. This has open up a whole world of new applications for smart cards.

The smart card is a multipurpose card and the same card can be used for a variety of functions: as an identity card, a door opener, a means to gain access to restricted areas; to operate vending machines, use the telephone, pay for bus tickets, go shopping, pay utility and insurance bills, photocopy, borrow books in the library, pay motorway tolls and parking, buy petrol, receive video on demand, download information on the PC, home shop, and more. The card can also be used to receive payments and information.

Smart cards have for some time been available and operational in parts of Europe. Banks in Norway, Denmark and Finland have been providing smart card services to their clients for several years. In Germany, smart cards are being used extensively in healthcare systems for patient information and billing. This successful healthcare application led the US Department of Defense to set up a trial using smart cards (GemPlus) for storage and transfer of medical health information. The entire bank payment system in France, involving 22 million people, has been converted to smart card technology.

There are two main reason why Europe is ahead of the United States in this development. First, in Europe there is a greater degree of government involvement providing support for investment, encouraging the process of standardisation and facilitating appropriate market regulation. Second, the high cost of telecommunication services in Europe compared to the United States has helped smart cards flourish amongst retailers who no longer has to carry the cost of expensive dial-up systems for authorisation of credit cards.[53]

So the conversion to smart card technology is already

happening and the massive replacement of cards and readers and refitting of equipment is gradually going ahead. "This technology is sneaking into our lives from the back door," according to Bob Gilson, executive director of the Smart Card Forum. The Smart Card Forum is an industry group with considerable influence, representing leading banks, retailers, equipment manufacturers, software companies and government agencies involved in the development of universal standards and regulatory frameworks for smart cards.

Both Visa and Mastercard have invested substantially in smart cards technology. Mastercard has a number of smart card services in Australia. Visa developed an experimental programme for the 1996 Atlanta Olympics involving the use of disposal smart cards. Visitors and participants were able to use the cards for all kinds of services. Visa is also working with Microsoft to develop smart card technology for networked information services. So 1996 was a year of prototyping and massive experimentation with smart card applications. All the major banks and card companies, software and electronics companies, many retailers and information providers were busy working with strategic alliances to pioneer new systems.

As far as investment in development of new transactional systems is concerned, it is clearly in the area of smart card technology that the most substantial investments are being made and also where the most significant developments are taking place.

Visa International, Mastercard International and Europay International have recently proposed "an industry standard for smart cards" – the EMV specification (named after the three companies), which no doubt will have a significant impact on future developments. This is based upon the already established ISO 7816 standard for smart cards. The EMV standard will rely on encryption technology to authenticate the user, keep data confidential and prevent data tampering.

Third-party clearing and brokering

Some companies are emerging in the market-place offering credit card clearance and marketing services for electronic commerce. They are basically leveraging the credit card system and acting as an intermediary between the vendor, the buyer and the bank. Some of these companies are dedicated to handling financial transactions for information assets being traded over open networks. First Virtual Holding is one such company which, in addition to offering a clearing and payment service, will market information assets on behalf of vendors in their own electronic shop on Internet.

The advantage with this model is that buyers do not have to send their credit card numbers over insecure networks. The financial transaction happens off-line or only online in secure networks. The service company may also allow transactions to accumulate in clients' accounts before settlement, making it possible also to use credit cards for smaller transactions. The disadvantage with this system is that it adds several steps to the information transaction process as well as an intermediary, which will have an impact on cost, profit and price.

Electronic cash

Over the last couple of years, a number of initiatives have appeared which attempt to develop solutions to the problems of facilitating transactions online over the open global networks. The argument is that the customer (the Internet surfer) should be able to shop and perform transactions instantly on his or her PC without having to wait for cheques to clear, or having to use a credit card or subscribe or have licensing arrangements with vendors.

The concept of "virtual money" has been introduced under many names, including eCash, CyberCash and NetCash. The idea is that customers will be able to approach "digital banks" on the Net which will issue electronic cash in exchange for real cash. It is a bit like buying tokens. The eCash tokens can be used for shopping with vendors which accept this form of token cash. The vendors will change the tokens back into real cash, through the same "digital bank" as the customer went to.

One company in Holland, DigiCash, has invested considerable resources in developing a system that aims to provide complete anonymity to individuals – the identity of the buyer is hidden through sophisticated use of encryption technology and the transactions are not traceable. This has serious implications for law enforcement and crime control. If transactions were allowed to be anonymous, it would open the flood-gates for criminal activity including money laundering, fraud and tax evasion.

The possibility of anonymous transaction systems for trading information assets is not very attractive to information providers, who depend on close communication with their customers and the ability to track information usage for marketing purposes as well as legal and financial reasons.

The initial attraction of electronic cash is that it seems more secure to shift tokens over the networks rather than real money. However, electronic cash tokens represents real money value and purchasing power. Consequently these proposed models for electronic cash can be perceived as being attempts to create new forms of currencies.

The likelihood of the world economy being receptive to new currencies that lack all the basic criteria of being able to grow value and operate financially is rather farfetched. For instance, electronic cash does not have any national reserve or guarantor – it does not belong in any national or international jurisdiction – and there is no way of earning real interest on eCash tokens. The task of creating a new global payment system is enormous and the task of introducing a new global currency is probably impossible. However, these experiments are evolving in a learning process and there may be many useful functions being developed on the way. New interesting solutions will no doubt come out of collaboration between these research-oriented initiatives and traditional players in the transactional market.

Electronic cheques

At the same stage of introductory experimentation are electronic cheques. There are a number of pilot projects investigating the use of electronic cheques in the form of encrypted email messages containing the digital signature of the payer. Most of these are envisaged to work with existing financial services. NetCheque is one such project developed at the University of South California. The user creates a cheque on screen using his or her digital signature, sending the electronic cheque as encrypted email. The recipient forwards it electronically to the bank, which receives it as an email order to transfer funds.

A problem with both electronic cash and electronic cheques is the lack of standards and guidelines. The market-place is currently exploding with many different initiatives based on a variety of different approaches and technology. The Internet user venturing into shopping on the network is likely to be well and truly confused and overwhelmed by the choices of payment systems being announced. Here is a list of electronic cash/cheque options currently available. Companies come and go every day in this business, so there is no guarantee that the names on this list will still be alive when you read it.

- ecash
- CyberCash
- NetCash
- Netchex
- NetBill
- Netcheque
- NetMarket
- NexusBucks
- LETSystems
- MagicMoney

Electronic Data Interchange (EDI)

EDI is a well-established system for exchanging sensitive data over networks. It is included in this context because since the extension of its current use could prove very interesting for conducting information transactions. Electronic data interchange (EDI) is defined as "The transfer of structured data, from computer to computer, using agreed communication standards."[54] The transfer of data is directly useable by the recipient's computer without the need to re-key data. EDI is an inter-organisational system involving two or more organisations, allowing the users to exchange standard trade documents such as orders, invoices, price lists, product catalogues, custom declaration forms, and so on.

EDI is based on a series of standards for exchanging data over communication and telephony networks, some of which are internationally ratified – the so-called EDIFACT standards. The major standard-setting body for commercial EDI applications is UN/EDIFACT (United Nations/EDI for Administration, Commerce and Transport). EDIFACT comprises of a set of internationally agreed standards, directions and guidelines for EDI and deals particularly with the trade in goods and services between independent computer systems and networks.

EDI has been around for many years and is growing very rapidly. Historically, various different industry groups got together and defined their own respective standards. For example, the car industry established the ODETTE-based system (Organisation for Data Exchange TeleTransmission in Europe) and the banks established the SWIFT network (Society for Worldwide Inter-bank Financial Telecommunications).

The European Commission has long recognised the strategic importance of EDI for improving trade relations in the European Union and stimulating economic growth. The Commission has launched a dedicated programme called TEDIS (Trade Electronic Data Interchange) to carry out research, and develop solutions that can fuel the uptake of EDI applications in European industry.

Several projects funded under this programme have demonstrated that EDI can be extended to the trading of information assets in electronic form and that EDI systems can be developed to handle the transfer of pictures, sound and multimedia as well as the existing alpha numerical information. EDI is currently mostly used by companies in closed networks. However, much research and experimentation is currently going on to explore new EDI applications linked to the commerce over open global networks.

The inherent ability of EDI to protect data, to track usage and audit information are all important features for an effective information transaction system. It is very likely that EDI will play an important role linked to transactional systems for trading information over networks. However, the high cost of European telecommunication services, ISDN and EDI software is currently a deterrent in many to implementing EDI.

Chapter 5
The way forward

> Make haste slowly
> Gaius Suetonius Tranquillus, c. AD 69–140

Summary of critical issues

Digital information transactions

Shifting money over digital networks is easy compared to the challenge of shifting information assets over the same networks. Money is tangible and instantly convertible into a fixed physical state. Money is very content poor, in fact the content of money is limited to globally accepted numbers and there is little ground for dispute concerning its value.

Information assets are very different. They are much less tangible and dynamic. They are content rich and content difficult. As established in the preceding chapters, a number of mechanisms need to be in place in order to facilitate transactions of different kinds of information assets over digital networks, mechanisms that will secure the protection of IPRs, the integrity and autheniticy of information, the identification of information, and the tracking and recording of information usage. There are also legal and political problems to be addressed. And the problem of pricing information assets in digital form for a global market is causing major headaches on the corporate level.

It is important to distinguish between electronic transactions for financial assets, goods and services, and electronic transactions that include online dissemination of information assets in electronic form, in particular IPR-protected assets. Systems available in the market-place today have so far been occupied with finding solutions to electronic financial transactions and not transactions integrating the simultaneous transaction of money and information.The question is, To what extent will these emerging systems be applicable and able to accommodate the online trade of information assets? They may be able to cope with transactions of information provided the assets are defined as "bulk products" such as books, films, videos, CDs, cassettes, journals and magazines. But how will they cope with the mass-distribution of "items of information" from a multitude of original sources to high volumes of very low-volume individual customers?

Changing markets and new business models

Publishers will have to rethink current business models that are based on the assumption that the market consumes all information packaged in bulk products. The scenario for trading assets over networks in the global information market allows for consumption on demand – the consumer will pay for actual information use. On-demand publishing requires new business models that will capitalise on the changes taking place in the market.

Some of the most significant changes in the buying behaviour of information consumers is that in a networked environment consumers are:

- much more selective, targeting the specific information they require;
- being aided by browsers, menus, indexes and search software;
- being served and (controlled) by intelligent agents, user profiling and information gatekeepers;
- expecting a high degree of functionality, for instance being able to interact with the information, compile and customise information from a variety of sources;
- wanting to obtain the information instantly; and
- increasingly only prepared to pay for actual use and wanting access to preview information and "try it on before they buy".

In order to take advantage of all the new opportunities for delivering information over networks, it will be essential to develop transactional systems that can deal efficiently with information assets delivered on demand and in fragmented and or compiled form, to a global customer base where individual buyers may represent very small transactions. The transactional systems which will survive in the future will have to be based on large-scale, low-cost, automated operations, near real-time clearance, and efficient settlement and be able to mass-process very small transactions.

Information identification and the protection of IPRs

Another growing requirement is the need to be able to use identification systems to mark and encode information, for the purpose of protecting intellectual property rights, secure authenticity and to track information usage. This is a very difficult area fraught with political and legal problems. There are currently many different projects around the world in different camps trying to develop information identifiers and standards for encoding information. It is premature to pass judgement on these developments as they are all on the drawing-board. But it is clearly an area that needs to be monitored very carefully.

Copyright protection and rights clearence

Copyrights have for centuries provided the economic foundation for the information trade. The development of digital technology and global networks has created many challenges for the copyright system. The concept of copyright has been expanded to accommodate the changes brought about by the digital revolution and the escalating growth of electronic use of published information. Critical work has been carried out and is still going on to develop the intellectual property system so that it will work as a vehicle for intellectual and economic growth in the future as well as it has in the past. Different types of information assets such as text, music, illustrations, video, multimedia programmes, databases, and so on all depend on legal protection to survive as tradeable commodities.

Another need being discussed is for systems that allow for rapid clearance of rights, such as electronic copyright management systems. Many multimedia developers are currently frustrated with the difficulty and high cost of clearing multiple rights from multiple sources. However, the need for efficient trading systems for rights should not be confused with notions of setting up huge central control-towers directing all the distributions of proceeds derived from licensing electronic rights. The introductions of any compulsory scheme or licensing model would have an adverse effect on the market. The process of marketing rights and designing and implementing IPR management systems should be left to the market-place to resolve.

There are several software packages available for individual companies to manage rights administration, and publishers, libraries and production companies are already using these tools to customise their rights management systems. Some collecting societies have also developed their own systems: for example, the Rapid Clearance Service from the Copyright Clearance Center (CCC) in the United States, and the Copyright Licensing Agency's Rapid Clearance System (CLARCS) in Britain. Several software companies are trying to build systems that will ride on top of existing rights clearance services with a view to facilitating one-stop shopping for the licensing of rights. There will be a number of prototypes and systems appearing in the market place over the next few years.

Security versus privacy

A problem largely ignored by many software developers is the use of high-grade encryption technology is heavily regulated: in many countries it is illegal to use and to export. The reason it is illegal is either because of national laws concerning national security and law-enforcement and/or because of national laws concerning data protection, privacy and consumer rights. Many of the proposed transaction systems, trade and management systems for IPRs include the use of encryption technology that is not legal in many jurisdictions. There is an urgent need to examine this activity and to review the current legal implications.

Technology is a two-edged sword – it can be used for good and bad purposes. Encryption technology can be used to secure the integrity of trade and cultural prosperity, but it can also be used as an instrument of criminal activity and unlawful behaviour. The monitoring, tracking, recording and coding of information can be used to produce better books and deliver more timely information, but it can also be used to invade people's privacy and put the individual under complete surveillance control at the mercy of those who are privileged to access his or her personal information profile.

The legal and regulatory jungle

One of the main challenges for achieving truly global transaction systems for information assets is to find a viable path in the overwhelming jungle of legal implications in different jurisdictions. Regulatory frameworks and different legal regimes are in conflict and competition with each other. There is, for instance, a tug of war between competition law and IPR – between national security and privacy, between standards and consumer rights. There is also considerable confusion with regard to liability and responsibility in the convergent media market. Who is liable for information services, for the content of the information assets being disseminated over networks – the carrier, the network operator, the service provider, the publisher, the author – and who is the publisher and the author of these compiled assets?

Traditional media and communication industries are subject to a complex regulatory framework. There are substantial differences in how these industries are regulated – for instance, the television industry is in most countries heavily regulated, while the press operates with a minimum of regulation, and functions on the principle of self-regulation. Which tradition and sets of principles are to be safeguarded in the networked information market?

These are crucial questions regarding regulatory issues that will have a profound impact on the success of the information trade and dictate many factors affecting the design of new transactional systems to facilitate this trade, as well as the trade itself.

Finally, the relaxation of cross-media ownership rules may be ill-conceived. It is intended to stimulate competition and achieve diversity, but it may prove to have just the opposite effect. The trend of market concentration and vertical integration is continuing – and there is a threat of market dominance by a few very large conglomerates controlling both carriers, networks, services and content.

Global information society versus information city states

We need to consider the long-term consequences of developing the global information society. This assessment must be balanced with an understanding of the social and political implications of the decisions we take. We live in a world of division – between the privileged few and the underprivileged many, between north and south, between the affluent and the starving. If we are not careful, the global information society will be reserved for those who can afford the membership fee. To ensure that access to the benefits of the wired world is open for all, we depend upon political intervention and commitment from our political leaders to develop and implement a public policy for the global information society. Otherwise, we could be heading towards a world of even greater division – where the gap between the knowledge-rich and the knowledge-poor will continue to widen. Some scientists are predicting that ten years from now, we shall live in a world governed by a network of global information city-states. The borders between these information hubs will have more significance than national borders. The individuals who will have access to these information networks will, at best, constitute one-eigth of the world's population – hardly a development that will foster democracy. Their message stands in sharp contrast to the message we hear from many of the wired world missionaries who would like us to believe that everyone will have access and that the stairway to heaven is to acquire an ever-growing range of information products.

The question we need to ask is what kind of society do we want – are our aspirations all democratic and truly global – or simply commercial and at best multinational? We have the opportunity to use the global information society and the potent power of a networked economy to help us deal with the biggest problems facing our world – the imbalance of wealth, unemployment, poverty, scarcity of resources, pollution, crime and wars. Are we aspiring towards creating a better world or are we satisfied with continued economic growth in the short term?

Conditions for market efficiency, and potential risks

A number of conditions need to be met for the information market to operate efficiently:

- open markets, free competition;
- diversity, choice and availability of information products wanted by consumers;
- clearly defined roles, responsibility and accountability;
- revision, updating and improvement of regulatory frameworks;
- harmonisation of competing legal regimes;
- international standards for information transaction, security and quality control;

- public policy initiatives to encourage and protect local creation of intellectual property; and
- government involvement to explore funding models for education, research, libraries and cultural heritage.

Failure to meet these conditions will undermine the development of the global information society. The risks involved are complex and far-reaching:

Less choice

If the market development is dominated by a few large media/information industry conglomerates, creating standards and acting as gatekeepers to information stores, the consumer could risk ending up with far less choice of information sources, price and technology than he or she has today.

Back to proprietary systems

If open systems take too long to achieve inter-operable standards, they will lose the battle with proprietary system vendors who are already in the market-place with solutions. Business cannot afford to wait for the ideal solution to emerge. If a proprietary system can do the job now rather than sometime tomorrow – then it does not matter to business if the system is proprietary.

Deregulation leading to monopolistic competition

If deregulation of the market means that cross-media ownership rules will be abolished or substantially changed, this may lead to less competition rather than more.

Lack of security

National security and law enforcement may be compromised by the increased use of encryption technology.

Infringement of privacy and consumer rights

Privacy and anonymity will be a thing of the past if many of the proposed technologies are implemented in the market. For the first time in history it will be possible through digital technology to monitor and control an individual's use of information on a scale never seen before. The risk of constant invasion of privacy and infringement of consumer rights is very real.

Loss of right to information access and universal service

Human rights principles of equal access for all to information and education are at stake in the new information economy. The cost of meeting the ambitions of international agreements on human rights that include the principle of providing a minimum universal service will be enormous. If governments do not hurry to define a new funding model for education, research, cultural and social welfare, then those rights will no longer exist. Information is already expensive and access to tomorrow's advanced multimedia services will be even more expensive.

There are many risks and threats to the development of a commercial information-based economy. These constitute both existing and potential barriers to trade. By examining the main conditions for market efficiency, it becomes apparent what those barriers are or may become. The process of harmonising national and international law, definitions of regulatory frameworks, political intervention, standards, technological constraints, competition and market dominance, are all important issues in this regard.

Barriers to overcome

The political commitment to, willingness to invest in, and enthusiasm for the global information society expressed by various government administrations around the world will no doubt boost the development of the world's information economy. However, President Jacques Santer's "vision of the information society as a road to human enrichment"[55] will only come true if these critical issues are resolved.

There are many obstacles to overcome. The so-called global information market is homogeneous neither in structure nor content. Any information asset owner who ventures into the electronic market-place will experience complications. The local markets which constitute the transnational market, are quite different in terms of legislation, public policy, market behaviour, level of technology and mechanisms in place to support a global information society.

There are complex problems concerning digital distribution of content and electronic information transactions. The success of trading information and media assets over global electronic networks will depend on the ability to facilitate secure information transactions and to protect intellectual property rights in an open, deregulated market environment.

There are competing legal regimes, conflicting sets of regulation and overlap in different laws, on both a national and an international level. The confusion concerning legal frameworks is not limited to intellectual property laws. There are also other regulatory frameworks affecting information transactions, standards, security, privacy, consumer rights, market competition and contract law. For instance, it may seem to be a sensible idea to implement encryption technology to facilitate secure transactions of information assets over digital networks. However, while this is legal for some industry sectors and in some countries obligatory for security purposes, in a number of countries it is illegal and a criminal offence to encode information using high-grade encryption technology.

Cross-media ownership rules are one example of a definite barrier to trade. But the way to overcome this should be to redesign those rules to stimulate competition and economic growth, not to throw out the whole concept or minimise the influence of those rules so they are reduced to no effect.

Publishers should be granted their long-awaited rights. Without them they are in a legal vacuum – the author has rights and the producer has rights – but so far the creative activities of the publishers have not yet been recognised and given rights. The lack of legal protection that the publisher suffers in this regard will become more of a disadvantage in electronic multimedia publishing and is likely to be a barrier to trade as the publishers will not have the economic incentive to release content on the networks.

Something needs to be resolved with regards to the role of collecting societies. However, to anticipate a standard for collective administration of copyright is very unrealistic. There are too many conflicting interests, different cultures, many rights and too many legal implications for that to happen. Rights are commercial commodities and the owners will certainly insist on controlling the administration of what are their core assets. Although rights clearance is clearly a barrier to trade for some players – such as multimedia developers – to other commercial interests it is not a barrier but a booming business.

The continued globalization of the information market requires harmonisation of different regulatory frameworks in order to secure legal protection of intellectual property on an international level. The convergence of technology, together with deregulation and concentration of the world market, are currently causing major problems in the legal domain where laws are applied based on national jurisdictions and industrial divisions. The mechanisms and principles for information transactions in the global information market will require a much more harmonised regulatory framework. A new legal map is needed to match the changing landscape. The current map does not fit the global information market. Harmonisation of laws and regulations is needed at both national and international levels, and between as well as within respective legal regimes, for instance intellectual property rights, fair competition, industry regulation, contract structures and licensing schemes.

Secure and efficient payment systems to facilitate transactions of information assets over electronic networks are essential, but they are not sufficient to persuade rights-holders to release content on to networks. Tools and mechanisms to track and record information usage, secure the integrity of information, verify users, identify copyright material and secure payment to rights-holders, are also essential to underpin the trading of information assets over networks.

Projections for future developments

The task of establishing projections for the future is very much constrained by the fact that there is wide disagreement on forecasting data. The projections given here are therefore based on a mixture of data interpretations, as well as an attempt to imagine the future gazing into that famous crystal ball.

It is difficult to predict future developments beyond what has already been hinted at. The experts and industry leaders who have been consulted in the process of writing this book have had some very different visions and expectations. However, market observations and investment figures would indicate that the trends of industry convergence and strategic alliances between previously separate industries will continue.

There is a shift emerging from companies focusing on "single purpose" products and market segmentation to companies focusing on service concepts, bundling products and services in attempt to lock in loyal customer groups.

As far as transactional technology is concerned, encryption technology seems set to develop a range of new mechanisms that will facilitate the trading of complex information assets, provided the legal barriers can be overcome.

Smart card technology will penetrate the market over the next decade and the executive wallet 15 years hence will be very slim indeed – maybe containing two or three smart cards and no cash. The smart card will also replace the driver's licence, ID cards and insurance certificates.

Anonymity will be an illusion, but confidentiality may survive if governments and regulators intervene in time.

Global IPR management systems will be in place five to ten years from now based on an infrastructure of many inter-operable systems, rather than large central facilities. Some will be collectively owned and some will be run by large media companies.

The trading of intellectual property rights will become much more market-oriented and media companies will discover many new ways of use/reuse of rights, optimising the value of their rights portfolios.

It will be more conducive to economic growth if the strategy and mechanisms for managing rights and transactions are left for competitive market forces to sort out, rather than governments seeking to force standards or introduce new regulation.

The individual citizen and the wired world

There are competing visions and very different expectations of what the wired world is all about. For the individual citizen it will bring change and new opportunities. There are valuable benefits to be enjoyed, but also less desirable consequences to deal with.

The private sector is beyond question the main driver behind the new networked economy and it is commercial enterprise that is pushing to bring you the magical connections to the wired world. Why? Because they want to sell you "stuff". Bill Gates, one of the most influential business men of our time sums it all up:

If you are watching the movie Top Gun and think Tom Cruise's aviator sunglasses look really cool, you'll be able to pause the movie and learn about the glasses or even buy them on the spot – if the film has been tagged with commercial information . . . if the movie star carries a handsome leather briefcase or handbag, the highway will let you browse the manufacturer's entire line of leather goods and either order one or be directed to a retailer.[56]

Twenty-four-hour screen shopping in the global supermarket, narcissistic obsessions with materially rich lifestyles, the polished superlooks of mass produced superstars and virtual imagery may go down well in the United States, but the idea that to be able to shop instantly on a scale never known before or to look like a movie star are the ultimate fruits of technological advance is a shallow idea. A quote from last century and Stephen Butler comes to mind: "Advertising may be described as the science of arresting human intelligence long enough to get some money from it."[57]

Connectivity to an ever-growing range of different activities and functions has the potential to change and enrich our lives is so many ways. It is up to the individual person, organisation and government to decide how best to make use of the powerful tools of a connected wired world.

It is true that there will always be cultural differences; what is perfectly acceptable and desirable in one culture will be rejected and frowned upon in another. Take the example of advertising in Europe, which is very different to advertising in the United States. In fact what works and what is acceptable varies greatly from country to country. People will have different objectives and agendas, different tastes and preferences in the old world.

There is much more to the global information society than a Global Super Shop. We must not limit the wonders of the global information society to a gigantic shopping venture. The existential notion of "I shop therefore I am" represents a kind of consumerist madness, which can have a corrupting and devastating effect upon the values of education, art, music, culture, and so on.

"I connect therefore I am" is another definition of Life which is apparent in today's wired world, where tools of technology seem more important than what can be achieved with original thought. We need to balance our investment in the global information society so that the individual citizen can enjoy the richness of human life today as well as in the future. It would be wise to recall the judgement of King Thamus described in the first chapter of this book. He warned his chief inventor about being blinded by enthusiasm for the new invention and unable to see the implications of what it could do to people and society. He pointed out the dangers of what might happen when people "receive a quantity of information without proper instruction" and when "they are filled with the conceit of wisdom, rather than real wisdom": people may appear to be knowledgeable, but be mostly ignorant and consequently a burden to society.

We most look beyond connectivity to a life of creativity. It is the intellectual capacity and creativity of the individual that will enable us to put the global information infrastructure to good use. People are needed to build the global information society – they are the core asset in the new networked economy – technology is not. Simply being connected to the grid of a wired world is of little value. Knowing what to do with the connection is the challenge.

The original existential notion of the French philosopher René Descartes read "I think therefore I am."

Appendix 1

Chapter 1 of the Bangemann Report,
*Europe and the Global Information Society:
Recommendations to the European Council*

In its Brussels meeting of December 1993, the European Council requested that a report be prepared for its meeting on 24–25 June 1994 in Corfu by a group of prominent persons on the specific measures to be taken into consideration by the Community and the Member States for the infrastructures in the sphere of information.

On the basis of this report, the Council will adopt an operational programme defining precise procedures for action and the necessary means.

Brussels, 26 May 1994

Chapter 1   The information society – new ways of living and working together

A revolutionary challenge to decision makers

Throughout the world, information and communications technologies are generating a new industrial revolution already as significant and far-reaching as those of the past.

It is a revolution based on information, itself the expression of human knowledge. Technological progress now enables us to process, store, retrieve and communicate information in whatever form it may take – oral, written or visual – unconstrained by distance, time and volume.

This revolution adds huge new capacities to human intelligence and constitutes a resource which changes the way we work together and the way we live together.

This revolution adds huge new capacities to human intelligence and . . . . changes the way we work together and the way we live together.

Europe is already participating in this revolution, but with an approach which is still too fragmentary and which could reduce expected benefits. An information society is a means to achieve so many of the Union's objectives. We have to get it right, and get it right now.

Partnership for jobs

Europe's ability to participate, to adapt and to exploit the new technologies and the opportunities they create, will require partnership between individuals, employers, unions and governments dedicated to managing change. If we manage the changes beforeus with determination and understanding of the social implications, we shall all gain in the long run.

Our work has been sustained by the conviction expressed in the Commission's White Paper, Growth, Competitiveness and Employment, that " . . . the enormous potential for new services relating to production, consumption, culture and leisure activities will create large numbers of new jobs . . . ". Yet nothing will happen automatically. We have to act to ensure that these jobs are created here, and soon. And that means public and private sectors acting together.

If we seize the opportunity

All revolutions generate uncertainty, discontinuity – and opportunity. Today's is no exception. How we respond, how we turn current opportunities into real benefits, will depend on how quickly we can enter the European information society.

In the face of quite remarkable technological developments and economic opportunities, all the leading global industrial players are reassessing their strategies and their options.

A common creation or a still fragmented Europe?

The first countries to enter the information society will reap the greatest rewards. They will set the agenda for all who must follow. By contrast, countries which temporise, or favour half-hearted solutions, could, in less than a decade, face disastrousdeclines in investment and a squeeze on jobs.

Given its history, we can be sure that Europe will take the opportunity. It will create the information society. The only question is whether this will be a strategic creation for the whole Union, or a more fragmented and much less effective amalgam of individual initiatives by Member States, with repercussions on every policy area, from the single market to cohesion.

The only question is whether this will be a strategic creation for the whole Union, or a more fragmented and much less effective amalgam of individual initiatives by Member States.

What we can expect for . . .

- Europe's citizens and consumers:
- A more caring European society with a significantly higher quality of life and a wider choice of services and entertainment.
- the content creators:
- New ways to exercise their creativity as the information society calls into being new products and services.
- Europe's regions:
- New opportunities to express their cultural traditions and identities and, for those standing on the geographical periphery of the Union, a minimising of distance and remoteness.
- governments and administrations:
- More efficient, transparent and responsive public services, clos-

er to the citizen and at lower cost.
- European business and small and medium sized enterprises:
- More effective management and organisation, access to training and other services, data links with customers and suppliers generating greater competitiveness.
- Europe's telecommunications operators:
- The capacity to supply an ever wider range of new high value-added services.
- the equipment and software suppliers; the computer and consumer electronics industries:
- New and strongly-growing markets for their products at home and abroad.

The social challenge

The widespread availability of new information tools and services will present fresh opportunities to build a more equal and balanced society and to foster individual accomplishment. The information society has the potential to improve the quality of life of Europe's citizens, the efficiency of our social and economic organisation and to reinforce cohesion.

The information society has the potential to improve the quality of life of Europe's citizens, the efficiency of our social and economic organisation and to reinforce cohesion.

The information revolution prompts profound changes in the way we view our societies and also in their organisation and structure. This presents us with a major challenge: either we grasp the opportunities before us and master the risks, or we bow to them, together with all the uncertainties this may entail.

The main risk lies in the creation of a two-tier society of have and have-nots, in which only a part of the population has access to the new technology, is comfortable using it and can fully enjoy its benefits. There is a danger that individuals will reject the new information culture and its instruments.

Such a risk is inherent in the process of structural change. We must confront it by convincing people that the new technologies hold out the prospect of a major step forward towards a European society less subject to such constraints as rigidity, inertia and compartmentalisation. By pooling resources that have traditionally been separate, and indeed distant, the information infrastructure unleashes unlimited potential for acquiring knowledge, innovation and creativity.

Mastering risks, maximising benefits

Thus, we have to find ways to master the risks and maximise the benefits. This places responsibilities on public authorities to establish safeguards and to ensure the cohesion of the new society. Fair access to the infrastructure will have to be guaranteed to all, as will provision of universal service, the definition of which must evolve in line with the technology.

A great deal of effort must be put into securing widespread public acceptance and actual use of the new technology. Preparing Europeans for the advent of the information society is a priority task. Education, training and promotion will necessarily playa central role. The White Paper's goal of giving European citizens the right to life-long education and training here finds its full justification. In order best to raise awareness, regional and local initiatives – whether public or private – should be encouraged.

Preparing Europeans for the advent of the information society is a priority task. Education, training and promotion will necessarily play a central role.

The arrival of the information society comes in tandem with changes in labour legislation and the rise of new professions and skills. Continuous dialogue between the social partners will be extremely important if we are to anticipate and to manage the imminent transformation of the work place. This concerted effort should reflect new relationships at the work place induced by the changing environment.

More detailed consideration of these issues exceeds the scope of this Report. The Group wishes to stress that Europe is bound to change, and that it is in our interest to seize this opportunity. The information infrastructure can prove an extraordinary instrument for serving the people of Europe and improving our society by fully reflecting the original and often unique values which underpin and give meaning to our lives.

At the end of the day, the added value brought by the new tools, and the overall success of the information society, will depend on the input made by our people, both individually and in working together. We are convinced that Europeans will meet this challenge.

Time to press on

Why the urgency? Because competitive suppliers of networks and services from outside Europe are increasingly active in our markets. They are convinced, as we must be, that if Europe arrives late our suppliers of technologies and services will lack the commercial muscle to win a share of the enormous global opportunities which lie ahead. Our companies will migrate to more attractive locations to do business. Our export markets will evaporate. We have to prove them wrong.

Tide waits for no man, and this is a revolutionary tide, sweeping through economic and social life. We must press on. At least we do not have the usual European worry about catching up. In some areas we are well placed, in others we do need to do more – but this is also true for the rest of the world's trading nations.

The importance of the sector was evident by its prominence during the Uruguay Round of GATT negotiations. This importance is destined to increase.

We should not be sceptical of our possibilities for success. We have major technological, entrepreneurial and creative capabilities. However, the diffusion of information is still too restricted andtoo expensive. This can be tackled quickly through regulatory reforms.

APPENDIX 1 155

Public awareness of the technologies has hitherto been too limited. This must change. Political attention is too intermittent. The private sector expects a new signal.

Political attention is too intermittent. The private sector expects a new signal.

An Action Plan

This Report outlines our vision of the information society and the benefits it will deliver to our citizens and to economic operators. It points to areas in which action is needed now so we can start out on the market-led passage to the new age, as well as to the agents which can drive us there.

As requested in the Council's mandate, we advocate an Action Plan based on specific initiatives involving partnerships linking public and private sectors. Their objective is to stimulate markets so that they can rapidly attain critical mass.

In this sector, private investment will be the driving force. Monopolistic, anticompetitive environments are the real roadblocks to such involvement. The situation here is completely different from that of other infrastructural investments where public funds are still crucial, such as transport.

This sector is in rapid evolution. The market will drive, it will decide winners and losers. Given the power and pervasiveness of the technology, this market is global.

The market will drive . . . the prime task of government is to safeguard competitive forces . . .

The prime task of government is to safeguard competitive forces and ensure a strong and lasting political welcome for the information society, so that demand-pull can finance growth, here as elsewhere.

By sharing our vision, and appreciating its urgency, Europe's decision-makers can make the prospects for our renewed economic and social development infinitely brighter.

New markets in Europe's information society

Information has a multiplier effect which will energise every economic sector. With market driven tariffs, there will be a vast array of novel information services and applications:

- from high cost services, whose premium prices are justified by the value of benefits delivered, to budget price products designed for mass consumption;
- from services to the business community, which can be tailored to the needs of a specific customer, to standardised packages which will sell in high volumes at low prices;
- from services and applications which employ existing infrastructure, peripherals and equipment (telephone and cable TV networks, broadcasting systems, personal computers, CD players and ordinary TV sets) to those which will be carried via new technologies, such as integrated broadband, as these are installed.

Markets for business

Large and small companies and professional users are already leading the way in exploiting the new technologies to raise the efficiency of their management and production systems. And more radical changes to business organisation and methods are on the way.

Business awareness of these trends and opportunities is still lower in Europe compared to the US. Companies are not yet fully exploiting the potential for internal reorganisation and for adapting relationships with suppliers, contractors and customers. We have a lot of pent up demand to fill.

Business awareness of these trends and opportunities is still lower in Europe compared to the US.

In the business markets, teleconferencing is one good example of a business application worth promoting, while much effort is also being dedicated worldwide to the perfection of telecommerce and electronic document interchange (EDI).

Both offer such cost and time advantages over traditional methods that, once applied, electronic procedures rapidly become the preferred way of doing business. According to some estimates, handling an electronic requisition is one tenth the cost of handling its paper equivalent, while an electronic mail (e-mail) message is faster, more reliable and can save 95% of the cost of a fax.

Electronic payments systems are already ushering in the cashless society in some parts of Europe. We have a sizeable lead over the rest of the world in smart card technology and applications. This is an area of global market potential.

Markets for small and medium sized enterprises

Though Europe's 12 million SMEs are rightly regarded as the backbone of the European economy, they do need to manage both information and managerial resources better.

They need to be linked to easy access, cost-effective networks providing information on production and market openings. The competitiveness of the whole industrial fabric would be sharpened if their relationships with large companies were based on the new technologies.

Networked relationships with universities, research institutes and laboratories would boost their prospects even more by helping to remedy chronic R&D deficiencies. Networking will also diminish the isolation of SMEs in Europe's less advantaged regions, helping them to upgrade their products and find wider markets.

Markets for consumers

These are expected to be richly populated with services, from home banking and teleshopping to a near-limitless choice of entertainment on demand.

In Europe, like the United States, mass consumer markets may emerge as one of the principal driving forces for the information society. American experience already shows that the development markets encounters a number of obstacles and uncertainties.

Given the initial high cost of new pay-per-view entertainment services, and of the related equipment, as well as the high cost of bringing fibre optics to the home, a large mass consumer market will develop more easily if entertainment services are part of a broader package. This could also include information data, cultural programming, sporting events, as well as telemarketing and teleshopping. Pay-per-view for on-line services, as well as advertising, will both be necessary as a source of revenue. To some extent, existing satellite and telephone infrastructure can help to serve the consumer market in the initial phase.

At the moment, this market is still only embryonic in Europe and is likely to take longer to grow than in the United States. There, more than 60% of households are tapped by cable TV systems which could also carry text and data services. In Europe, only 25% are similarly equipped, and this figure masks great differences between countries, e.g. Belgium (92%) and Greece (1–2%).

Another statistic: in the United States there are 34 PCs per hundred citizens. The European figure overall is 10 per hundred, though the UK, for instance, at 22 per hundred, is closer to the US level of computer penetration.

Lack of available information services and poor computer awareness could therefore prove handicaps in Europe. Telecommunication networks are, however, comparable in size and cover, but lag behind in terms of utilisation. These networks, therefore, can act as the basic port of access for the initial services, but stimulation of user applications is still going to be necessary.

Such structural weaknesses need not halt progress. Europe's technological success with CD-ROM and CD-I could be the basis for a raft of non-networked applications and services during the early formative years of the information society. These services on disk have considerable export potential if Europe's audio-visual industry succeeds in countering current US dominance in titles.

In terms of the market, France's Minitel network already offers an encouraging example that European consumers are prepared to buy information and transaction services on screen, if the access price is right. It reaches nearly 30 million private and business subscribers through six million small terminals and carries about 15,000 different services. Minitel has created many new jobs, directly and indirectly, through boosting business efficiency and competitiveness.

In the UK, the success of the Community-sponsored Homestead programme, using CD-I, is indicative, as is the highly successful launch of (an American) dedicated cable teleshopping channel.

Meanwhile in the US, where the consumer market is more advanced, video-on-demand and home shopping could emerge as the most popular services.

Audio-visual markets

Our biggest structural problem is the financial and organisational weakness of the European programme industry. Despite the enormous richness of the European heritage, and the potential of our creators, most of the programmes and most of the stocks of acquired rights are not in European hands. A fast growing European home market can provide European industry with an opportunity to develop a home base and to exploit increased possibilities for exports.

Linguistic fragmentation of the market has long been seen as a disadvantage for Europe's entertainment and audio-visual industry, especially with English having an overwhelming dominance in the global market – a reflection of the US lead in production and, importantly, in distribution. This lead, which starts with cinema and continues withtelevision, is likely to be extended to the new audio-visual areas. However, once products can be easily accessible to consumers, there will be more opportunities for expression of the multiplicity of cultures and languages in which Europe abounds.

. . . once products can be easily accessible to consumers, there will be more opportunities for expression of the multiplicity of cultures and languages in which Europe abounds.

Europe's audio-visual industry is also burdened with regulations. Some of these will soon be rendered obsolete by the development of new technologies, hampering the development of a dynamic European market.

As a first step to stimulating debate on the new challenges, the Commission has produced a Green Paper on the audio-visual industry.

Appendix 2

Speech of US Vice President Al Gore at the International –Telecommunications Union's first World Telecommunication Development Conference, Buenos Aires, March 1994

I have come here, 8,000 kilometers from my home, to ask you to help create a Global Information Infrastructure. To explain why, I want to begin by reading you something that I first read in high school, 30 years ago.

"By means of electricity, the world of matter has become a great nerve, vibrating thousands of miles in a breathless point of time . . . The round globe is a vast . . . brain, instinct with intelligence!"

This was not the observation of a physicist – or a neurologist. Instead, these visionary words were written in 1851 by Nathaniel Hawthorne, one of my country's greatest writers, who was inspired by the development of the telegraph. Much as Jules Verne foresaw submarines and moon landings, Hawthorne foresaw what we are now poised to bring into being.

The ITU was created only 14 years later, in major part for the purpose of fostering an internationally compatible system of telegraphy.

For almost 150 years, people have aspired to fulfill Hawthorne's vision – to wrap nerves of communications around the globe, linking all human knowledge.

In this decade, at this conference, we now have at hand the technological breakthroughs and economic means to bring all the communities of the world together. We now can at last create a planetary information network that transmits messages and images with the speed of light from the largest city to the smallest village on every continent.

I am very proud to have the opportunity to address the first development conference of the ITU because the President of the United States and I believe that an essential prerequisite to sustainable development, for all members of the human family, is the creation of this network of networks. To accomplish this purpose, legislators, regulators, and businesspeople must do this: build and operate a Global Information Infrastructure. This GII will circle the globe with information superhighways on which all people can travel.

These highways – or, more accurately, networks of distributed intelligence – will allow us to share information, to connect, and to communicate as a global community. From these connections we will derive robust and sustainable economic progress, strong democracies, better solutions to global and local environmental challenges, improved health care, and – ultimately – a greater sense of shared stewardship of our small planet.

The Global Information Infrastructure will help educate our children and allow us to exchange ideas in within a community and among nations. It will be a means by which families and friends will transcend the barriers of time and distance. It will make possible a global information marketplace, where consumers can buy or sell products. I ask you, the delegates to this conference, to set an ambitious agenda that will help all governments, in their own sovereign nations and in international cooperation, to build this Global Information Infrastructure. For my country's part, I pledge our vigorous, continued participation in achieving this goal – in the development sector of the ITU, in other sectors and in plenipotentiary gatherings of the ITU, and in bilateral discussions held by our Departments of State and Commerce and our Federal Communications Commission.

The development of the GII must be a cooperative effort among governments and peoples. It cannot be dictated or built by a single country. It must be a democratic effort.

And the distributed intelligence of the GII will spread participatory democracy.

To illustrate why, I'd like to use an example from computer science.

In the past, all computers were huge mainframes with a single processing unit, solving problems in sequence, one by one, each bit of information sent back and forth between the CPU and the vast field of memory surrounding it. Now, we have massively parallel computers with hundreds – or thousands – of tiny self-contained processors distributed throughout the memory field, all interconnected, and together far more powerful and more versatile than even the most sophisticated single processor, because they each solve a tiny piece of the problem simultaneously and when all the pieces are assembled, the problem is solved.

Similarly, the GII will be an assemblage of local, national, and regional networks, that are not only like parallel computers but in their most advanced state will in fact be a distributed, parallel computer.

In a sense, the GII will be a metaphor for democracy itself.

Representative democracy does not work with an all-powerful central government, arrogating all decisions to itself. That is why communism collapsed.

Instead, representative democracy relies on the assumption that the best way for a nation to make its political decisions is for each citizen – the human equivalent of the self-contained processor – to have the power to control his or her own life.

To do that, people must have available the information they need. And be allowed to express their conclusions in free speech and in votes that are combined with those of millions of others. That's what guides the system as a whole.

The GII will not only be a metaphor for a functioning democracy, it will in fact promote the functioning of democracy by greatly enhancing the participation of citizens in decision-making. And it will greatly promote the ability of nations to cooperate with each other. I see an new Athenian Age of democracy forged in the fora the GII will create.

The GII will be the key to economic growth for national and

international economies. For us in the United States, the information infrastructure already is to the US economy of the 1990s what transport infrastructure was to the economy of the mid-20th century.

The integration of computing and information networks into the economy makes US manufacturing companies more productive, more competitive, and more adaptive to changing conditions and it will do the same for the economies of other nations.

These same technologies are also enabling the service sectors of the US economy to grow, to increase their scale and productivity and expand their range of product offerings and ability to respond to customer demands.

Approximately 60% of all US workers are "knowledge workers" – people whose jobs depend on the information they generate and receive over our information infrastructure. As we create new jobs, 8 out of 10 are in information-intensive sectors of our economy. And these new jobs are well-paying jobs for financial analysts, computer programmers, and other educated workers.

The global economy also will be driven by the growth of the Information Age. Hundreds of billions of dollars can be added to world growth if we commit to the GII. fervently hope this conference will take full advantage of this potential for economic growth, and not deny any country or community its right to participate in this growth.

As the GII spreads, more and more people realize that information is a treasure that must be shared to be valuable. When two people communicate, they each can be enriched – and unlike traditional resources, the more you share, the more you have. As Thomas Jefferson said, "He who receives an idea from me, receives instruction himself without lessening mine; as he who lights his taper at mine, receives light without darkening me."

Now we all realize that, even as we meet here, the Global Information Infrastructure is being built, although many countries have yet to see any benefits.

Digital telecommunications technology, fiber optics, and new high-capacity satellite systems are transforming telecommunications. And all over the world, under the seas and along the roads, pipelines, and railroads, companies are laying fiber optic cable that carries thousands of telephone calls per second over a single strand of glass.

These developments are greatly reducing the cost of building the GII. In the past, it could take years to build a network. Linking a single country's major cities might require laying thousands of kilometers of expensive wires. Today, a single satellite and a few dozen ground stations can be installed in a few months – at much lower cost.

The economics of networks have changed so radically that the operation of a competitive, private market can build much of the GII. This is dependent, however, upon sensible regulation.

Within the national boundaries of the US we aspire to build our information highways according to a set of principles that I outlined in January in California. The National Information Infrastructure, as we call it, will be built and maintained by the private sector. It will consist of hundreds of different networks, run by different companies and using different technologies, all connected together in a giant "network of networks," providing telephone and interactive digital video to almost every American.

Our plan is based on five principles: First, encourage private investment; Second, promote competition; Third, create a flexible regulatory framework that can keep pace with rapid technological and market changes; Fourth, provide open access to the network for all information providers; and Fifth, ensure universal service.

Are these principles unique to the United States? Hardly. Many are accepted international principles endorsed by many of you. I believe these principles can inform and aid the development of the Global Information Infrastructure and urge this Conference to incorporate them, as appropriate, into the Buenos Aires Declaration, which will be drafted this week.

Let me elaborate briefly on these principles.

First, we propose that private investment and competition be the foundation for development of the GII. In the US, we are in the process of opening our communications markets to all domestic private participants.

In recent years, many countries, particularly here in Latin America, have opted to privatize their state-owned telephone companies in order to obtain the benefits and incentives that drive competitive private enterprises, including innovation, increased investment, efficiency and responsiveness to market needs.

Adopting policies that allow increased private sector participation in the telecommunications sector has provided an enormous spur to telecommunications development in dozens of countries, including Argentina, Venezuela, Chile, and Mexico. I urge you to follow their lead.

But privatization is not enough. Competition is needed as well. In the past, it did make sense to have telecommunications monopolies.

In many cases, the technology and the economies of scale meant it was inefficient to build more than one network. In other cases – Finland, Canada, and the US, for example – national networks were built in the early part of this century by hundreds of small, independent phone companies and cooperatives.

Today, there are many more technology options than in the past and it is not only possible, but desirable, to have different companies running competing – but interconnected – networks, because competition is the best way to make the telecommunications sector more efficient, more innovative – and more profitable as consumers make more calls and prices decline.

That is why allowing other companies to compete with AT&T, once the world's largest telephone monopoly, was so useful for the United States. Over the last ten years, it has cut the cost of a long-distance telephone call in the US more than 50%.

To promote competition and investment in global telecommunications, we need to adopt cost-based collection and accounting rates. Doing so will accelerate development of the GII.

International standards to ensure interconnection and interoperability are needed as well. National networks must connect effectively with each other to make real the simple vision of linking schools, hospitals, businesses, and homes to a Global Information Infrastructure.

Hand in hand with the need for private investment and competition is the necessity of appropriate and flexible regulations developed by an authoritative regulatory body.

In order for the private sector to invest and for initiatives opening a market to competition to be successful, it is necessary to create a regulatory environment that fosters and protects competition and private sector investments, while at the same time protecting consumers' interests.

Without the protection of an independent regulator, a potential private investor would be hesitant to provide service in competition with the incumbent provider for fear that the incumbent's market power would not be adequately controlled.

Decisions and the basis for making them must also be made public so that consumers and potential competitors are assured that their interests are being protected.

This is why in the US, we have delegated significant regulatory powers to an independent agency, the Federal Communications Commission. This expert body is well-equipped to make difficult technical decisions and to monitor, in conjunction with the National Telecommunications and Information Administration and the department of Justice, changing market conditions. We commend this approach to you.

We need a flexible, effective system for resolution of international issues, too – one that can keep up with the ever-accelerating pace of technological change.

I understand that the ITU has just gone through a major reorganization designed to increase its effectiveness. This will enable the ITU, under the able leadership of Mr. Tarjanne, to streamline its operations and redirect resources to where they are needed most. This will ensure that the ITU can adapt to future and unimaginable technologies.

Our fourth principle is open access. By this I mean that telephone and video network owners should charge non-discriminatory prices for access to their networks. This principle will guarantee every user of the GII can use thousands of different sources of information – video programming, electronic newspapers, computer bulletin boards – from every country, in every language.

With new technologies like direct broadcast satellites, a few networks will no longer be able to control your access to information – as long as government policies permit new entrants into the information marketplace.

Countries and companies will not be able to compete in the global economy if they cannot get access to up-to-date information, if they cannot communicate instantly with customers around the globe. Ready access to information is also essential for training the skilled workforce needed for high-tech industries.

The countries that flourish in the twenty-first century will be those that have telecommunications policies and copyright laws that provide their citizens access to a wide choice of information services.

Protecting intellectual property is absolutely essential.

The final and most important principle is to ensure universal service so that the Global Information Infrastructure is available to all members of our societies. Our goal is a kind of global conversation, in which everyone who wants can have his or her say.

We must ensure that whatever steps we take to expand our worldwide telecommunications infrastructure, we keep that goal in mind.

Although the details of universal service will vary from country to country and from service to service, several aspects of universal service apply everywhere. Access clearly includes making service available at affordable prices to persons at all income levels. It also includes making high quality service available regardless of geographic location or other restrictions such as disability.

Constellations of hundreds of satellites in low earth orbit may soon provide telephone or data services to any point on the globe.

Such systems could make universal service both practical and affordable.

An equally important part of universal access is teaching consumers how to use communications effectively. That means developing easy-to-use applications for a variety of contexts, and teaching people how to use them. The most sophisticated and cost-efficient networks will be completely useless if users are unable to understand how to access and take full advantage of their offerings.

Another dimension of universal service is the recognition that marketplace economics should not be the sole determinant of the reach of the information infrastructure.

The President and I have called for positive government action in the United States to extend the NII to every classroom, library, hospital, and clinic in the US by the end of the century.

I want to urge that this conference include in its agenda for action the commitment to determine how every school and library in every country can be connected to the Internet, the world's largest computer network, in order to create a Global Digital Library. Each library could maintain a server containing books and journals in electronic form, along with indexes to help users find other materials. As more and more information is stored electronically, this global library would become more and more useful.

It would allow millions of students, scholars and businesspeople to find the information they need whether it be in Albania or Ecuador.

Private investment . . . competition . . . flexibility . . . open access . . . universal service.

In addition to urging the delegates of this conference to adopt these principles as part of the Buenos Aires Declaration, guiding the next four years of telecommunications development, I assure you that the US will be discussing in any fora, inside and outside the ITU, whether these principles might be usefully adopted by all countries.

The commitment of all nations to enforcing regulatory regimes to build the GII is vital to world development and many global social goals.

But the power of the Global Information Infrastructure will be diminished if it cannot reach large segments of the world population.

We have heard together Dr. Tarjanne's eloquent speech setting forth the challenges we face. As he points out: the 24 countries of the OECD have only 16 percent of the world's population. But they account for 70 percent of global telephone mainlines and 90 percent of mobile phone subscribers.

There are those who say the lack of economic development causes poor telecommunications. I believe they have it exactly backwards. A primitive telecommunications systems causes poor economic development.

So we cannot be complacent about the disparity between the high and low income nations, whether in how many phones are available to people or in whether they have such new technologies as high speed computer networks or videoconferencing.

The United States delegation is devoted to working with each of you at this Conference to address the many problems that hinder development.

And there are many. Financing is a problem in almost every country, even though telecommunications has proven itself to be an excellent investment.

Even where telecommunications has been identified as a top development priority, countries lack trained personnel and up-to-date information.

And in too many parts of the world, political unrest makes it difficult or impossible to maintain existing infrastructure, let alone lay new wire or deploy new capacity.

How can we work together to overcome these hurdles? Let me mention a few things industrialized countries can do to help.

First, we can use the Global Information Infrastructure for technical collaboration between industrialized nations and developing countries.

All agencies of the US government are potential sources of information and knowledge that can be shared with partners across the globe.

The Global Information Infrastructure can help development agencies link experts from every nation and enable them to solve common problems. For instance, the Pan American Health Organization has conducted hemisphere-wide teleconferences to present new methods to diagnose and prevent the spread of AIDS.

Second, multilateral institutions like the World Bank, can help nations finance the building of telecommunications infrastructure.

Third, the US can help provide the technical know-how needed to deploy and use these new technologies. USAID and US businesses have helped the US Telecommunications Training Institute train more than 3500 telecommunications professionals from the developing world, including many in this room.

In the future, USTTI plans also to help businesspeople, bankers, farmers, and others from the developing world find ways that computer networking, wireless technology, satellites, video links, and other telecommunications technology could improve their effectiveness and efficiency.

I challenge other nations, the development banks, and the UN system to create similar training opportunities.

The head of our Peace Corps, Carol Bellamy, intends to use Peace Corps volunteers both to help deploy telecommunications and computer systems and to find innovative uses for them. Here in Argentina, a Peace Corps volunteer is doing just that.

To join the GII to the effort to protect and preserve the global environment, our Administration will soon propose using satellite and personal communication technology to create a global network of environmental information. We will propose using the schools and students of the world to gather and study environmental information on a daily basis and communicate that data to the world through television.

But regulatory reform must accompany this technical assistance and financial aid for it to work. This requires top-level leadership and commitment – commitment to foster investment in telecommunications and commitment to adopt policies that ensure the rapid deployment and widespread use of the information infrastructure.

I opened by quoting Nathaniel Hawthorne, inspired by Samuel Morse's invention of the telegraph.

Morse was also a famous portrait artist in the US – his portrait of President James Monroe hangs today in the White House. While Morse was working on a portrait of General Lafayette in Washington, his wife, who lived about 500 kilometers away, grew ill and died. But it took seven days for the news to reach him.

In his grief and remorse, he began to wonder if it were possible to erase barriers of time and space, so that no one would be unable to reach a loved one in time of need. Pursuing this thought, he came to discover how to use electricity to convey messages, and so he invented the telegraph and, indirectly, the ITU.

The Global Information Infrastructure offers instant communication to the great human family.

It can provide us the information we need to dramatically improve the quality of their lives. By linking clinics and hospitals together, it will ensure that doctors treating patients have access to the best possible information on diseases and treatments. By providing early warning on natural disasters like volcanic eruptions, tsunamis, or typhoons, it can save the lives of thousands of people.

By linking villages and towns, it can help people organize and work together to solve local and regional problems ranging from improving water supplies to preventing deforestation.

To promote . . . to protect . . . to preserve freedom and democracy, we must make telecommunications development an integral part of every nation's development. Each link we create strengthens the bonds of liberty and democracy around the world. By opening markets to stimulate the development of the global information infrastructure, we open lines of communication.

By opening lines of communication, we open minds. This summer, from my country cameras will bring the World Cup Championship to well over one billion people.

To those of you from the 23 visiting countries whose teams are in the Finals, I wish you luck – although I'll be rooting for the home team.

The Global Information Infrastructure carries implications even more important than soccer.

It has brought us images of earthquakes in California, of Boris Yeltsin on a tank in Red Square, of the effects of mortar shells in Sarajevo and Somalia, of the fall of the Berlin Wall. It has brought us images of war and peace, and tragedy and joy, in which we all can share.

There's a Dutch relief worker, Wam Kat, who has been broadcasting an electronic diary from Zagreb for more than a year and a half on the Internet, sharing his observations of life in Croatia.

After reading Kat's Croatian diary, people around the world began to send money for relief efforts. The result: 25 houses have been rebuilt in a town destroyed by war.

Governments didn't do this. People did. But such events are the hope of the future.

When I began proposing the NII in the US, I said that my hope is that the United States, born in revolution, can lead the way to this new, peaceful revolution. However, I believe we will reach our goal faster and with greater certainty if we walk down that path together. As Antonio Machado, Spanish poet, once said, "Pathwalker, there is no path, we create the path as we walk."

Let us build a global community in which the people of neighboring countries view each other not as potential enemies, but as potential partners, as members of the same family in the vast, increasingly interconnected human family.

Let us seize this moment. Let us work to link the people of the world. Let us create this new path as we walk it together.

Appendix 3

Documents on the information society and infrastructure released by national governments, the European Commission and G7 countries

Australia

Networking Australia's Future, December 1994, Broadband Services Expert Group

Canada

The Canadian Information Highway: Building Canada's Information and Communication Infrastructure, April 1994

Denmark

Info-society 2000, November 1994

European Commission

White Paper on Growth, Competitiveness and Employment, 1994

Europe and the Global Information Society: Recommendation to the European Council, Bangemann Group, 26 May 1994

Europe's Way to Information Society: An Action Plan. European Commission, 19 July 1994

Green Paper on the Liberalisation of Telecommunications Infrastructures and Cable Television Networks, part II, 1994

Green Paper on Intellectual Property and the Global Information Society, published by the European Commission, August 1995.

France

Les autoroutes de l'information, Gérard Théry, 1994

Germany

Multimedia: Chance und Herausforderung (Multimedia: opportunities and challenges), March 1995, Bundesministerium für Bildung, Wissenschaft, Forschung und Technologie

Japan

Reforms toward the Intellectual Creative Society of the 21st Century: Programme for the Establishment of High-performance Info-communications Infrastructures, 31 May 1994, Telecommunications Council, Ministry of Post and Telecommunications

Programme for Advanced Information Infrastructure, May 1994, Ministry of International Trade and Industry

The Netherlands

Actieprogramma Elektronische Snelwegen – van Metafoor naar Actie (Action programme electronic highways – from metaphor to action), December 1994

Norway

Norwegian Information Infrastructure, March 1994

Innspill til Norsk Bidrag til Informasjons-infrastruktur (Proposal for a Norwegian contribution to the information infrastructure), January 1995

Singapore

Ministry of Information, Singapore, *Information Technology 2000: A Vision of an Intelligent Island*, March 1992.

Sweden

Information Technology: Wings to Human Ability, August 1994

United Kingdom

Creating the Superhighways of the Future: Developing Broadband Communications in the UK, November 1994

United States

The National Information Infrastructure: Agenda for Action, 15 September 1993

National Information Infrastructure: Progress Report, September 1993–1994

Global Information Infrastructure: Agenda for Co-operation, February 1995

White Paper on Intellectual Property and the Global Information Infrastructure, US Department of Commerce, July 1995.

G7

G7 Ministerial Conference on the Information Society: Theme Paper, Brussels, 23 January 1995

Chair's Conclusions Issued by the G7 Ministers, 27 February 1995

Notes

1 Brian Murphy, *The World Wired Up*, Comedia, 1983, p.11.
2 Minna Antrim, quoted in *Collins Dictionary of Quotations*, Collins, 1995.
3 Reader's Digest, *Dictionary of Essential Knowledge*, 1995.
4 Morse tried unsuccessfully to secure patents in Europe and there were many legal disputes over the claims of ownership of the telegraph invention. There were several scientists and engineers in different corners of the world who contributed to the development of the telegraph.
5 Marshall and Eric McLuhan, *Laws of the Media*, University of Toronto Press, 1988.
6 Plato, *Phaedrus*, quoted by N. Postman, *Technopoly*, Vintage Books, 1993, p. 4.
7 Op. cit., p. 5.
8 Interview with Nicholas Negroponte by Joia Shillingford, *Financial Times*, IT Review, 6 March 1996, p II.
9 Robert Browning, "Death in the Desert".
10 Alvin Toffler, *Future Shock*, Random House, 1970, p. 31.
11 *The Concise Oxford Dictionary*, Oxford University Press, 1991.
12 International Trade Administration, US Department of Commerce, *Industrial Outlook 1994*, 25-1, January 1994.
13 International Trade Administration, US Department of Commerce, Office of Service Industries, 1994.
14 Al Gore, keynote address at the G7 Conference on the Global Information Society, Brussels, 27 February 1995.
15 *The Global Information Infrastructure: Agenda for Co-operation.*
16 Al Gore firmly established the concept of the GII with his speech at the

ITU's first World Telecommunication Development Conference in Buenos Aires in March 1994. There is a copy of this speech in the Appendices.
17 Position Paper of Clinton Campaign, 1992.
18 "The Economy", Bill Clinton campaign speech, Wharton School of Business, University of Pennsylvania, Philadelphia, 16 April 1992.
19 Speech by Larry Irving, head of National Telecommunications and Information Administration, US Department of Commerce, "Constructing the National Information Infrastructure: Ensuring that All Americans Get Connected", at the Vermont Telecommunications Forum, Winooski Park, Vermont, 20 March, 1995.
20 Chaired by Ronald H. Brown, then US Secretary of Commerce.
21 Chaired by Larry Irving, head of National Telecommunications and Information Administration of the US Department of Commerce.
22 Chaired by Sally Katzen, head of the Office of Information and Regulatory Affairs at the Office of Management and Budget (OMB).
23 Chaired by Arati Prabhakar, Director of the National Institute of Standards and Technology.
24 "The Global Information Infrastructure: Agenda for Cooperation" report from Ronald H. Brown, US Secretary of Commerce, Version 1.0.
25 Commission of the European Communities, *White Paper on Growth, Competitiveness, and Employment: The Challenges and Ways Forward into the 21st Century*, 5 December 1993.
26 Ichiya Nakamura, Directory Posts and Telecommunication International, "Development of the Info-Communication Infrastructure in Japan", paper presented at the International Publishers Association's Copyright Congress, Torino 23–25 May 1994.
27 Source: UNDP *Human Development Report*, 1993.
28 Ashok Bhojwani, "Information Strategies for the World: A Response from the Developing World", paper presented at the International Publishers Association's Copyright Congress, Torino, 23–25 May 1994.
29 Intercast is a system for providing interactive television services using existing analogue TV signals. The service was launched on 20 June 1996 and is backed by the Intercast Industry Group, established 23 October 1995.
30 For a detailed history of Internet, see for instance: Ed Krol, *The Whole*

Internet, O'Reilly and Associates, 1994.
31 Statement from Denis Gilhooly, Director Media and Technology, Wall Street Journal Europe, CEO Summit Meeting, Oxford, 7 April 1995.
32 Ibid.
33 John Patrick of IBM, speaking at the World Internet Conference in London, June 1996.
34 Statement from David Shaw MP, Conservative Party conference, July 1996.
35 Statement from Sir David Puttnam speaking at a seminar on the Global Information Society facilitated by the Oxford–Templeton Forum for Leaders of Industry and Government, at Templeton College, Oxford University, 13 May 1996.
36 Benjamin Gomes-Casseres, "Group Versus Group: How alliance Networks Compete", *Harvard Business Review*, vol. 72, July–August 1994, p. 62.
37 Speech delivered at the Networked Economy Conference, Paris 28 February, 1995.
38 Statement from Sir David Puttnam speaking at a seminar on the Global Information Society facilitated by the Oxford–Templeton Forum for Leaders of Industry and Government, at Templeton College, Oxford University, 13 May 1996.
39 There are intellectual property rights attached to defined categories of information and these rights are owned by the rights-holder, but the information itself cannot be owned in legal terms.
40 "Towards Realisation of the Information Society", discussion paper, Directorate for Science, Technology and Industry, OECD, March 1995.
41 The "tangible" vs the "intangible" is a central issue of debate in the field of intellectual property, since both are required in order for an "intellectual property" to succeed in the market.
42 John H. Gibbons, *Intellectual Property Rights in an Age of Electronics and Information*, Robert E. Krieger Publishing,1986, p. 21.
43 Ibid, p. 22.
44 Paul Goldstein, "Copyright", *Journal of the Copyright Society of the USA*, vol. 38, no. 3, 1991, pp. 109–22.
45 Lawrence Becker, "The Moral Basis of Property Rights", *Property*, J. Roland Penwork, 1980, pp. 189–90.
46 Paul Goldstein, op. cit., p. 110.

47 L. Ray Patterson and Stanley W. Lindberg, *The Nature of Copyright*, University of Georgia Press, 1991, pp. 20–21.
48 Gavin McFarlane, *A Practical Introduction to Copyright*, Waterlow, 1989, p. 2.
49 L. Ray Patterson and Stanley W. Lindberg, op. cit., pp. 123–40.
50 For example, Microsoft Network, hampered by US export regulations on encryption technology, and Netscape, hampered by French law, which does not allow the use of their encryption technology.
51 Peter N. Backe, *Industry for High-Grade Personal Computer Encryption Technology in Germany and the USA*, Oxford University, March 1995.
52 Eric Hughes, "A Long-term Perspective on Electronic Commerce", *Release 1*, March 1995.
53 Phil Patton, "E-money", *Popular Science*, July 1995.
54 Joe Peppard, *IT Strategy for Business*, Longman, 1993, p. 145.
55 Jacques Santer, President of the European Commission, statement from speech delivered at the fifth annual Networked Economy conference in Paris, 28 February 1995.
56 Bill Gates, *The Road Ahead*, Viking Penguin, 1995, p. 165.
57 Leacock Stephen Butler, *Collins Dictionary of Quotations*, Collins, 1995.

Select bibliography

Backe P.N., "Industry for high-grade personal computer encryption technology in Germany and the USA", MPhil thesis, Oxford University, 1995.
Becker L., "The moral basis of property rights", in *Property*, Roland Penvork,1980.
Stewart B., *The Media Lab*, Penguin Books, 1988.
Epper K., "A player goes after the big bucks in cyberspace", *American Banker*, vol. clx, no. 86, May 5 1995.
Gates B., *The Road Ahead*, Viking-Penguin, 1995.
Goldstein P., "Copyright", *Journal of the Copyright Society of the USA*, vol. 38, no. 3, 1991.
Gomes-Casseres B, "Group versus group: How alliance networks compete", *Harvard Business Review*, vol. 72, July–August 1994.
Hughes E., "A long-term perspective on electronic commerce", *Release*, vol. 1, no. 31, March 1995.
Katsh E., *Law in a Digital World*, Oxford University Press, 1995.
Keet E.E., *Preventing Piracy*, Addison Wesley, 1985.
Krol E., *The Whole Internet*, O'Reilly & Associates, 1994.
McFarlane G., *Copyright*, Waterlow,1989.
McLuhan M. and E., *Laws of Media*, University of Toronto Press, 1988.
Negroponte N., *Being Digital*, Hodder & Stoughton, 1995.
Patterson L.R. and Lindberg, S.W., *The Nature of Copyright*, University of Georgia Press, 1991.
Patton P., E-money, *Popular Science*, July 1995.

Peppard J., *IT Strategy for Business*, Longman, 1993.
Postman N., *Technopoly*, Vintage Books, 1993.
Toffler A., *The Third Wave*, Pan Books, 1981.
The Internet Letter, vol. 2, no. 2.

Legal and political documents:
Ministry of Information, Singapore, *Information Technology 2000: A Vision of an Intelligent Island*, March 1992.
Commission of the European Communities, *White Paper on Growth, Competitiveness, and Employment: The Challenges and Ways Forward into the 21st Century*, 5 December 1993.
Speech of US Vice President Al Gore at the International Telecommunications Union's first World Telecommunication Development Conference, Buenos Aires, March 1994.
The Global Information Infrastructure: Agenda for Co-operation, report from Ronald H. Brown, US Secretary of Commerce, version 1.0.
Bangemann Report, *Europe and the Global Information Society: Recommendations to the European Council*, 26 May 1994.
"Towards realisation of the information society", discussion paper, Directorate for Science, Technology and Industry, OECD, March 1995.
EC Software Directive – Council Directive 91/250.
EC Rental and Lending Directive – Council Directive 92/100.
EC Satellite and Cable Directive – Council Directive 93/83/EE.
EC Database Directive – Council Directive 95/464.
Green Paper on the Liberalisation of Telecommunications Infrastructures and Cable Television Networks, part II, 1994
White Paper on Intellectual Property and the Global Information Infrastructure, US Department of Commerce, July 1995.

Glossary

ATM: Asynchronous Transfer Mode. A packet-switching system and communication protocol for high-speed transfer of high volume data in telecommunication networks, making use of existing cables and network infrastructure.

ASDL: Asymmetric Digital Subscriber Line. A system which boosts signals and reduces the noise in telecommunication traffic in existing copper wire networks thereby increasing the capacity of telecommunication networks.

CD-ROM: compact disc read-only memory.

CD-I: compact disc interactive.

Clipper chip: on the 16 April 1993, a US Presidential initiative announced the introduction of a "Key-Escrow chip" which supposedly would provide secure telecommunications and networks without compromising law enforcement interests and national security. It was envisaged that the chip would be implemented in all communication devices sold in the United States. The chip is based on a classified symmetrical algorithm called Skipjack developed by the National Security Agency, many times more secure than DES or RSA. Government agencies have the ability to decrypt the data being encrypted by the clipper chip as they hold a decryption key for every chip sold together with information on who the devices were sold to. The intention with the clipper chip was to resolve the tension between the Government's need to protect national security and law enforcement interests and the users, need for privacy and security. The proposed scheme has not been well received in the market.

Cryptography: the science of encrypting/decrypting data and information, including principles, methods and mechanisms.

Decryption: a method of decoding encrypted data, restoring it to its original form.

DES: Data Encryption Standard. A single key algorithm adopted by NIST for public use. Widely used, but considered less secure than public key cryptography.

Digital signature: a string of encrypted digital values representing the identity of the sender and/or source of data, allowing the receiver to verify sender and/or data authenticity. The longer the encryption key the more secure the signature. Most keys are 512-bit, but encryption experts recommend 1024-bit keys.

DVD: digital versatile disc. A high-density optical digital compact disc which is available in a number of different formats based on internationally proposed standards' specifications:

DVD-ROM: digital versatile disc – read only memory. A high density version of CD-ROM.

DVD-Video: digital versatile disc – video. Non-recordable video disc intended for use with TV sets as a playback facility for films (comparable to video cassettes, except you cannot record on the DVD-Video discs).

DVD-Audio: a better high density version of the digital audio compact disc.

DVD-WO: digital versatile disc – write once. A version of the DVD-ROM which can be used for making recordings, but only once.

DVD-RAM: digital versatile disc – random access memory. A re-writeable high density optical disc intended as an integral PC component for the purpose of using multimedia/high volume data – a high capacity PC hard disc.

DVD-E: digital versatile disc – erasable. A fully recordable optical disc – the digital equivalent of a video cassette.

DVI: Digital video interactive. A version of the CD-ROM which has a limited capacity for storing video using compression techniques.

EC: European Commission.

EDI: Electronic Data Interchange Encryption. A method of coding and transforming data to an unintelligible state so it cannot be accessed in its original form.

EU: European Union.

FCC: Federal Communications Commission (United States).

GII: global information infrastructure.

GIM: global information market.

GIS: global information society.

GSM: global special mobile. An international industry standard for digital mobile telephony which is widely adopted in Europe and increasingly worldwide, except in the United States.

HTML: Hyper Text Mark-up Language. A standard format for hypertext files on the Internet/WWW developed by the Internet Engineering Task Force(IETF).

HTTP: HyperText Transfer Protocol. A standard format for data transfers over Internet/WWW developed by the Internet Engineering Task Force (IETF).

hypertext: a method of structuring data, linking text to other related texts in a collection of material.

ICT: information and communication technologies.

IDEA: International Data Encryption Algorithm.

Intelligent agent: a software programme which works as an automated information gathering tool. The programme has the capability to process information about individual users and their specific information requirements. The programme "learns" about users' particular search patterns and subject interests and uses this information to adapt the tool to individual users: that is why it is called "intelligent". The intelligent agent acts upon your instructions – go and find this information for me – and travels (surfs the Net) within and across databases and networks to get the information for you.

ISO: International Organisation for Standardisation, comprising members being national standards organisations.

ITU: International Telecommunication Union. An organisation under the administration of the United Nations dealing with telecommunications and standards.

Internet: a global system of many open interconnected computer networks.

ISBN: International Standard Book Number. A worldwide standard system for identifying and registering book publications.

ISSN: International Standard Serial Number. A worldwide standard system for identifying and registering journals.

ISDN: Integrated Subscriber Digital Network. An industry standard and a protocol for transferring voice and data over telecommunication networks.

IP: Internet Protocol. A communication protocol that lets packets of data traverse multiple networks on its way to its final destination.

JPEG: Joint Photographic Experts Group. A collaboration between ITU and ISO do develop standards for compression of continuous-tone still images.

key: a series of computer instructions that controls the process of encryption and decryption.

MHEG: Multimedia and Hypermedia information coding Experts Group. An ISO group which works on the development of standards for bit-stream specifications for multimedia and hypermedia applications.

MPEG: Motion Picture Experts Group. An ISO group working on the development of standards for storage and retrieval of video and audio in digital media.

MUD: multi-user domain.

NASA: National Aeronautics and Space Administration (United States).

the Net: slang referring to the Internet, the information highway or the global information infrastructure.

NII: *national information infrastructure.*

NTSC: National Television Systems Committee. One of the world's

GLOSSARY 187

three incompatible analogue colour video standards for instance used in United States, Canada and Japan, the other two being PAL and SECAM (used in France). NTSC is the inferior standard giving a poorer resolution of video images: maximum 525 lines per image as opposed to 625 lines available in PAL. See also PAL and SECAM.

PAL: Phase Alteration Line. Analogue colour video standard, used in most of Europe, Australia, Africa and South America. See also NTSC and NTSC.

PDA: personal digital assistant.

PGP: Pretty Good Privacy. A software program developed by P. Zimmermann and available free in the public domain over Internet. The program is used to encrypt and decrypt messages and data sent over Internet.

RSA: Rivest-Shamir-Adleman cipher. A comprehensive set of public-key- based cryptographic algorithms developed since 1977 at Massachusetts Institute of Technology, named after the inventors. Several RSA algorithms are protected (not in Europe) by US patents held by the PKP (Public Key Partners) company formed jointly by MIT and Stanford.

SECAM: Systeme Electronique Couleur Avec Memoire. Analogue colour video standard, developed and used in France. See NTSC and PAL.

S-HTTP: Secure HyperText Transfer Protocol. Security technology proposed as a standard for Internet.

SGML: Standard Generalised Mark-up Language. An ISO standard for the marking content and structuring content for electronic use.

SSL: Secure Socket Layer. Proprietary security technology developed by Netscape and proposed as a standard for Internet.

STM: Scientific, Technical and Medical (publishing).

TCP: Transmission Control Protocol (followed the IP Protocol) .*VLSI*: very large scale integration.

VR: virtual reality.

VRML: virtual reality mark-up language.

Web: slang referring to the World Wide Web (WWW).

WIPO: World Intellectual Property Organisation.

WTO: World Trade Organisation (previously GATT (General Agreement on Tariffs and Trade)).

WWW: World Wide Web. A networked system for organising information on the Internet, which uses hypertext links.